BEHOLD
YOUR GOD

Books in the Woman's Workshop Series

Behold Your God: Studies on the Attributes of God by Myrna Alexander

Designed by God: Studies on Healing and Wholeness by Kirkie Morrissey

Faith: Studies on Living the Christian Life by Martha Hook

Forgiveness by Kirkie Morrissey

The Fruit of the Spirit: Studies on Galatians 5:22–23 by Sandi Swanson

Greater Love: Studies on Friendship by Jean Shaw

Growing Godly: Studies on Bible Women by Diane Brummel Bloem

Heart Trouble: Studies on Christian Character by Barbara Bush

Loving and Obeying God: Studies on 1 Samuel by Myrna Alexander

Mastering Motherhood by Barbara Bush

Open Up Your Life: Studies on Christian Hospitality by Latayne C. Scott

People In Turmoil: A Woman's Workshop on First Corinthians by Carolyn Nystrom and Margaret Fromer

Perfect In His Eyes: Studies on Self-Esteem by Kay Marshall Strom

Talking With God: Studies on Prayer by Glaphré

Time, Talent, Things: Studies on Christian Stewardship by Latayne C. Scott

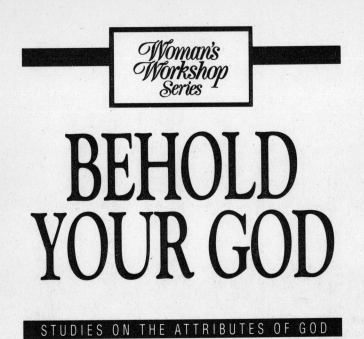

Woman's Workshop Series

BEHOLD YOUR GOD

STUDIES ON THE ATTRIBUTES OF GOD

MYRNA ALEXANDER

ZondervanPublishingHouse

Grand Rapids, Michigan

A Division of HarperCollinsPublishers

To my husband,
who took time to instruct
me in the Word of God.

CONTENTS

PREFACE

To come alive spiritually we must meet God.
To live abundantly we must *know* God.

Is knowing God practical to the daily life of a woman?
Yes! If *peace* is practical . . .
   "Acquaint now thyself with [thy God], and be at peace"
      (Job 22:21, KJV).
If *inner freedom* is practical . . .
   "You will know the truth, and the truth will make you
      free" (John 8:32).
If *understanding* is practical . . .
   "Knowledge of the Holy is understanding" (Prov. 9:10,
      KJV).
If being *strong* is practical . . .
   "The people who know their God shall be strong and do
      great things" (Dan. 11:32, KJV).

Even more basic, knowing God is essential for biblical faith, and faith is necessary for life as a Christian. "The just shall live *by faith*" (Rom. 1:17, KJV). "We walk *by faith,* not by sight" (2 Cor. 5:7).

Have you ever thought, "What I need is more faith"?

Faith is not a warm, positive feeling you need to "get." Faith is giving mental assent to something. It is making a decision to trust, lean, or depend upon someone or something. Therefore, faith never exists alone. Faith always has an object. You have faith *in* a chair to hold you up. You have faith *in* your husband, *in* your friend, *in* God. How you perceive the object of your faith will determine your actions. It is difficult to place your faith in someone or something about which you know little. Realistic faith involves, then, "a knowing." Knowing the chair will hold you up, you sit in it. Knowing the character of your husband or friend, you are led to trust him or not.

Biblical faith involves trusting in God alone. But here is the struggle: faith involves a "knowing" and few of us know much about the character of our God, especially in terms relevant to our daily lives. To consistently lean on God alone, we must know Him. To know Him, we must know what He is like. Discovering for ourselves the amazing truth of what God is like encourages us to place our faith in Him.

Since faith is the method for living the abundant Christian life, it would seem logical that the study of the character of God should be woven into the discipling of even the newest believer. Far too often such a study has been thought appropriate only for the theologian or seminary student. For this writer, the study of the character of God had far too long appeared impersonal, remotely abstract, hardly relevant to the everyday life of a homemaker. What a paradox when such a study is instead the practical source of faith's life for the Christian.

Should this paradox seem strange? Have not the Great Deceiver's attacks always been against the character of the almighty God? From his first approach to Eve to his most recent thrust into your life, Satan has desired to throw a curtain of doubt over the magnificent character of our God. God does not want us to be deceived. Therefore, He has revealed what He is like through the Holy Scriptures and through His Son, Jesus Christ.

A visionary picture of the character of God accompanied God's commissioning services of the prophets. The resulting concept of the person of God in their hearts became their stability in desperate times. No matter what the pressure, these servants of God stood firm, for they knew their God.

Today God challenges us to view Him in His Word. Those who do will be transformed. Thus, nothing could be more vital and practical to your Christian life than the personal discoveries and application of what God has revealed concerning Himself in His Word. The purpose, therefore, of this series is twofold. *First, to guide you to discover in the Scriptures truth concerning what God is like. Second, to encourage the practical translation of these truths into your life as a woman.*

Each lesson will consider the person of Jesus Christ, for "He reflects the glory of God and bears the very stamp of his nature. He is the image of the invisible God. . . . In Christ there is all of God in a human body. . . . He who has seen me has seen the Father" (Heb. 1:3; Col. 1:15; 2:9, LB; John 14:9).

Also, it is through the intimacy of a relationship with the person of Jesus Christ that all that God is becomes more than truth on a page and becomes alive in daily experience. Through Christ, all that God is, is in fellowship with the Christian.

HOW TO USE THIS STUDY BOOK

This study was originally written for a group of women who desired to study the Bible together in some depth. The study was designed to help guide these women into God's Word on a daily basis. There was a specific reason for the study preparation for each week's Bible study. Having known the joy and transforming growth in Christ that comes from daily study in the scriptures, the author finally realized that individual study is the key to group Bible studies where the goal is to see lives change. Listening to a Bible teacher is not enough; it is necessary that participants all share in the discovery process so that biblical truth might be digested personally.

Great growth and personal encouragement took place in this original group because the members came together prepared by the scriptures to interact upon God's principles. The results of personal research was shared in the group weekly. The need to share the product of study seems a valid need that results in growth. It is an important motivator for study and thereby encourages the development of habitual study of God's Word. Also, without participant preparation, Bible studies may degenerate into a "pooling of ignorance."

Serious and productive study involves commitment. This study guide is designed to demand consistent and serious study in order that fruitful and life changing discussion might be generated. The work of personal Bible study always bears joy and eternal results. To encourage the consistent habit of Bible study, the lessons are intended to be done on a regular basis: a discovery section a day; a lesson a week. However, the format may take different forms depending upon the group or individual using the material.

Ways the material could be used are:

1. *Women's Bible study in the local church:* The study should perhaps be done on a weekly basis to encourage an awareness of the character of God in the women so that they might grow in their life of faith. A suggested format for using this study with a large group might be:

   a. Coffee fellowship time (15 minutes).
   b. Opening, singing, and a testimony related to the application of the previous week's lesson to life (15 minutes).
   c. Discussion in small groups over the questions for the week (40 minutes). A small group would consist of eight to twelve people.
   d. Lecture summarizing the material studied and drawing applications (35 minutes).

2. *Small home, neighborhood, or business groups:* Though the format above is suggested for a larger church group, the material is designed to be adaptable to any size group whether it meets in a home, a neighborhood, or at work. Since each Bible study lesson is divided into five discovery sections, it is possible to divide the material as the group's time permits. For instance, a group of businesswomen might meet daily before their job and take one discovery each morning, completing one lesson a week. On the other hand, a group of

mothers in a neighborhood that meet once a week with their children present may find they are able to discuss only two or three discoveries a week, finishing a complete lesson every other week.

No matter how the material is used by a particular group, it is highly recommended that someone take the lead each time the group meets, whether that leadership rotates or remains with one person. The leader suggestions at the end of the book may be helpful to this person.

3. *Individual study or devotions:* Though originally used by a group, the study was also written for individuals who were unable to attend the weekly meeting but desired to use the study for their own daily devotions.

1

INTRODUCTION

The small child asks, "What is God Like?" The mother answers, "Well, God is kind of like . . . well, . . ."

A correct view of what God is like is at the core of the abundant life Jesus Christ promised in John 10:10. But what comes into your mind when you think of what God is like? Often God becomes a composite of all the religious pictures we've ever seen, added to the most wonderful people we've ever known, plus a powerful comic-book superman with a halo. We tend to reduce God to superhuman if not human terms. This is not surprising, for we are limited by what a human mind can conceive, and God is not exactly like anybody or anything. God is unique past all knowledge. There cannot be an all-inclusive definition given of God, for He is incomprehensible.

Do you realize we could not have known God except that *He* chose to make Himself known to us? God has revealed some of His personal qualities or characteristics. These qualities are often referred to as the "attributes of God." An attribute is something that is true of God. God's revelation of His character (His attributes) through creation, the Scriptures, and His Son, Jesus Christ, is *His* reply to our question, "What are You like?"

God wants us to know Him because He has created us for a personal, intimate relationship with Himself. For any relationship to exist, those involved must share some knowledge of each other. The more intimate the knowledge, the more personal the relationship becomes. God *knows* you to the smallest detail of your life; things you couldn't even know about yourself, He knows. (Read Psalm 139.) But what do you know about Him? God's desire is that you be increasing in the knowledge of Him. He has chosen to reveal Himself that we might know Him and thus share in the life-changing relationship of eternal life.

As we study what God is like, that we might come to know Him and live daily in an increasingly more vital relationship with Him, there is something we need to keep in mind. There is a danger in discussing the attributes of God, for we might begin to view the inexhaustible person of God as a mere list of characteristics!

When we experience a close relationship with our husbands, for example, we normally do not view their character as segmented . . . here is his love, over here his patience, there his kindness. We see our husband whole, as a person, not a piece of kindness added to a bit of patience. We live in a relationship with a person, not with a list of characteristics that reflect that person.

At times, however, we are asked, "What is your husband like?" Then we may explain our husband's character in fragments: "He is patient, kind, calm, stable." Our husbands are so much more than lists of characteristics, yet the characteristics give clues to what they are like.

Just so, as each lesson emphasizes a particular truth concerning the person of God, continually remember that God cannot be divided into parts. God is one, complete and perfect. It is to an intimately alive, all-encompassing relationship with the King of Kings and Lord of Lords that we are called.

Discovery I/Why Do You Need to Know What God Is Like?

The Scriptures reveal the amazing effect the knowledge of God will have on our lives as women. In the following verses, discover what characteristics will increasingly become true of you as you come to know your God.

1. a. What does Daniel 11:32 state will become true of one who knows God? (Make it personal; put your own name in the verse as you read it aloud.) _____

   _____

   b. Daniel 3:8-30 is an illustration of the truth you just discovered. What did the *application* of their knowledge of God enable the three men in this passage to do? _____

   _____

   _____

   c. In what area of your life do you need strength to stand firm? According to Daniel 11:32, how is that need to be met? _____

   _____

   _____

2. a. Name another effect the knowledge of God has on your life, as seen in Job 22:21; Isaiah 26:3; and Ephesians 2:14. _____

   b. In what circumstances do you lack peace? According to these verses, is it possible for you to have peace? How? _____

   _____

_____

_____

3. a. Proverbs 9:10 states another important reason we need to know God. What does this verse reveal?_____
   b. In what do you especially sense your need for this characteristic in your life?_____
4. a. A woman who knows God shall become (John 8:32).
   b. The apostle Paul Illustrated this effect in his own life when he declared _____ (Rom. 7:19,24-25).
   c. In what areas do you desire this evidence of knowing God in your life? _____

_____

_____

Discovery II/A View of God

5. Why has God chosen to reveal Himself to you? (See introductory section.) _____

_____

_____

6. How do people often view God (Ps. 50:21)? _____

_____

7. Why do you think people conceive of God as did the man in this psalm? _____

_____

_____

8. Describe in some detail how you conceive of God at the present time. (Be honest; this will be helpful to you later.)

_____

_____

_____

_____

Discovery III/The Correct View of God

9. Where do we find correct answers to our questions concerning what God is like?_____

   a. Psalm 19:1_____

   b. John 5:39_____

   c. John 14:9; 2 Corinthians 4:6; Colossians 1:15 _____

   _____

Discovery IV/The Attributes of God

10. What is an "attribute" of God? (See introductory section.)

    _____

11. Why is God *not* a composite list of characteristics? ___

    _____

    _____

12. In each of the following references, what do you discover about God?

    a. Deuteronomy 7:9; Lamentations 3:22-23_____

    b. 1 Chronicles 29:11-12_____

    _____

    _____

    c. Psalm 62:11 _____

    d. Psalm 90:2; Deuteronomy 33:27 _____

    e. Psalm 136:1 _____

    f. Psalm 139:2-4; John 21:17_____

    g. Psalm 139:7 _____

h. Daniel 4:35; 2 Chronicles 20:6_____

i. Malachi 3:6; Hebrews 13:8 _____

j. John 3:16; 1 John 4:16_____

13. Review your discoveries in question 2. Do you feel you could trust a God like this? Why?_____

_____

_____

_____

Discovery Lesson V/Personal Application of What You Have Learned

14. a. Think of an important issue *now* confronting you. Name it.

   b. Now look back at what you found to be true of God in question 12.

      1) God is_____

      2) God is_____

   c. Look at your circumstance or problem through the character of God. How might you specifically relate these truths concerning what God is like to your situation? _____

   _____

   _____

   d. Has your mental attitude concerning your situation been altered? How?_____

   _____

   _____

   e. Begin to practice looking at the daily joys, frustrations, and irritations of your life through the character of God. For example, unexpected company are arriving for dinner. You are not prepared, and your day is already packed with activities.

Alternative one: Panic.

Alternative two: View your circumstance through the character of God: 1) that God is in control of the company's arrival and has allowed them to come; 2) that God is good and therefore has planned good to come out of this event; 3) that God is all-powerful and so can empower you to accomplish all that is needed. ... And so on through what you know about God.

2

GOD IS LOVE

What would it be like to be loved by someone whose love for you is not influenced by anything you ever did, are now doing, or will do; whose love could never weaken or fluctuate? You can know what it would be like! For God's love for you is not influenced by anything you ever did or will do (Deut. 7:6-8; 2 Tim. 1:9). His love is unconditional. God chose to love you, and the moment He did, His personal love and happiness became identified or "tied up" with you (Ps. 104:31). You became the object of His affection, "the apple of [His] eye" (Ps. 17:8). Love does not exist in a vacuum. It must express itself, so God desired to express Himself to you through a personal relationship made possible by the death and resurrection of Jesus Christ.

The love God has for you will never change. He loves you as much today as when He gave His Son for you (Gal. 2:20; Titus 2:13-14), and He will keep on "giving" in love to you (Rom. 8:32). God's love will never weaken or fluctuate, for in Him "there is no variation or shadow due to change" (James 1:17). His personal love for you is eternal; thus, He loved you before you had any being, with a love that is everlasting (Jer. 31:3).

Though God's love has deep emotion, it is always holy and pure, never sentimental. He is not afraid to discipline us when we need to be redirected for our best good. (Heb. 12:6).

When you progressively come to "know and believe the love that God has toward [you]," you experience increasingly your freedom in Christ.

For example, responding by faith to God's love expressed in the Cross, and accepting His Son as your Savior, sets you free from sins that have entrapped or "guilt-haunted" you. (Rev. 1:5). Once you have accepted God's gift of His Son, you are not only set free from all sins past, present, and future, but from the present power of sin in your life. The temptation to be irritable, impatient, angry, and self-indulgent need no longer control you (Rom. 6).

Another liberating effect of the love of God on your life involves the issue of fear. Have you been afraid of God or of what God might allow to happen in your life? The Scriptures answer your concern with the cross of Christ, the supreme evidence of God's love for you. "Since he did not spare even his own Son for us but gave him up for us all, won't he also surely give us everything else?" (Rom. 8:32, LB). Fear surfaces when we feel that we may be harmed or made to suffer. For a moment, imagine someone who loves you. Picture this same person with all knowledge to know what is best for you and all power to allow only this best to take place in your life. Could you be afraid of such a one? Would you fear what this person might be "planning" for you? The nature of God's love causes Him to always desire what is best for you. The fact that He controls all things enables Him to accomplish His desire. No wonder resting your faith in this "perfect love casts out all fear" (1 John 4:18).

The realization that God loves you can satisfy your basic

need for self-worth. Consider the sense of worth you might experience should you discover that you are cherished and loved as closest friend to a president or king. But wonder of wonders, you are loved by the King of Kings and Lord of Lords, the Creator of all things, the One of whom the Scriptures declare:

> Thine, O Lord, is the greatness, and the power, and the glory, and the victory, and the majesty; for all that is in the heavens and in the earth is thine; thine is the kingdom, O Lord, and thou art exalted as head above all (1 Chron. 29:11).

This One loves you! You are of supreme value as a person, for now you are loved by God. In fact, you are loved so much that God gave His own Son in order to establish a relationship with you. Why worry what people think of you, for God is for you. He loves you; and "if God is for us, who is against us?" (Rom. 8:31).

God's love can radically affect your life in yet another unbelievable way. When you believe in Jesus Christ, the Spirit of God comes to literally live inside of you (Rom. 8:9; John 14:17) to enable you to live the new life of love for which you were created (1 Cor. 16:14).

"God's love has been poured into our hearts through the Holy Spirit which has been given to us" (Rom. 5:5). You, then, have God's love inside of you to empower you to "love one another" (1 John 4:11), to truly love your husband and your children (Titus 2:4), your friends and your enemies, as well as the ultimate joy of responding in love to Him who first loved you!

Discovery I/God's Love

1. Discover how God's love is described in the following verses, and write out the various descriptions in a personal way. (A dictionary may help you.) *Example:* God's love for me is "steadfast" (fixed, settled, constant).

    a. Psalm 106:1 _____

    b. Jeremiah 31:3 _____

    c. Romans 5:8 _____

    d. Romans 8:35-39 _____

    e. 1 Corinthians 13:4-7 _____

    f. Ephesians 3:19 _____

2. a. Discover various physical ways God demonstrates His love to the world and reflect upon these as ways God is showing you love today (Ps. 145:15-16; Matt. 5:45; Acts 14:17). _____

_____

_____

    b. How do you show love in physical ways to your family? to others? _____

_____

_____

_____

3. Love is not only expressed physically but also involves the feelings. Explain how 1 Corinthians 13:4-7 suggests that God's love for you has emotion and is personal. _____

_____

_____

Discovery II/God's Supreme Demonstration of Love

4. In the following verses, discover what God's personal love moved Him to do for you, and the specific reasons God expressed His love in this manner.

    a. John 3:16 _____

    b. 1 John 4:9-10 _____

c. Revelation 1:5_____

5. a. According to Romans 5:6-8; Ephesians 2:8-9; and 2
   Timothy 1:9, did you in any way earn or deserve this
   life-giving demonstration of God's love? _____

   _____

   b. How have you responded to God's supreme demonstration of love for you?_____

   _____

   _____

6. a. Once you have become a child of God, how "much"
   does God love you (John 17:23)? _____

   _____

   b. Rewrite this verse in your own words, putting your
   name in place of "them."_____

   _____

   _____

   c. What does this mean to you?_____

   _____

   _____

Discovery III/Unconditional Love

7. a. Jesus Christ gave the parable of the prodigal son (Luke
   15:11-32) to illustrate God's love. See if you can discover at least three aspects of the love of God revealed
   through this parable. _____

   _____

   _____

   _____

   b. Do you think the father in the parable continued to
   love the son when he left home? If so, what in the

parable gives you this idea? _____

_____

_____

8. a. Look up in a dictionary the word *unconditional* and then explain what the phrase "unconditional love" might mean. _____

_____

_____

   b. In light of this lesson, would you say God's love for His children is "conditional" at all by their actions?_____

_____

9. a. After Jesus Christ was taken by the Roman soldiers, His disciples denied and forsook Him (Matt. 26:56; Luke 22:54-62). What was His response to them (John 13:1)?_____

_____

   b. In what ways could this be an example to you?_____

_____

_____

10. Can anything you do or anything others do to you or any situation keep God from loving you? Consider Romans 8:35-39 and John 13:1. _____

_____

Discovery IV/God's Love Expressed
To and Through the Believer

11. Explain some of the ways God expresses love to His children, according to the following verses:

    a. Psalm 68:19 _____

    b. Romans 5:5_____

    c. Ephesians 1:3 _____

    d. Colossians 1:12-14 _____

    e. Hebrews 12:6 _____

12. Why might beginning to understand the love of God enable 1 John 4:18 to be experienced in your life? ____

_____

_____

13. a. Name one "result" of God's coming to live inside you (Rom. 5:5). _____

      _____

   b. On the basis of this truth, to what great ministry can God call His children (John 13:34; 1 Cor. 16:14)?

      _____

   c. Can you think of several specific persons to whom you may be especially called to minister in this way? ____

      _____

      _____

      _____

   d. As wives and mothers, we are to _____

      _____

      (Titus 2:4).

   e. What has God done to enable you to be obedient to this ministry (John 7:37-39; Rom. 5:5; Gal. 5:22)?

      _____

14. Think of a person you find difficult to love.

   a. Is it God's will for you to love that person? (Consider question 13). _____

      _____

   b. If you ask God to enable you to love this person, of

what two things can you be assured on the basis of 1 John 5:14-15? _____

_____

_____

c. The situation or your "feelings" may or may not change immediately, but what is to be your confidence? (2 Cor. 5:7)? _____

_____

Discovery V/Biblical Illustration of a
Man Who "Learned" to Love

15. Give a brief character sketch of the apostle John from reading the following: Mark 3:17; 10:35-45; Luke 9:51-56. _____

_____

_____

_____

16. Later in life, this same man wrote 1 John 4:7-21.
    a. According to this passage, what is John's great desire for his fellow believers? _____

    _____

    b. What do you think has caused this transformation?

    _____

    _____

17. What changes have progressively taken place in your life since God placed His love in *your* heart? _____

_____

_____

3

GOD IS SUPREME AND SOVEREIGN

"Thine, O LORD, is the greatness, and the power, and the glory, and the victory, and the majesty: for all that is in the heavens and in the earth is thine; thine is the kingdom, O LORD, and thou art exalted as head above all" (1 Chron. 29:11).

The love of God expressed through the gift of His Son is seen in striking relief against the brilliance of God's majesty and supremacy. God is supreme; and therefore, He is in control of all things (sovereign). "The Lord reigns; he is robed in majesty" (Ps. 93:1). With this truth as his basis, Job may proclaim: "I know that thou canst do all things, and that no purpose of thine can be thwarted" (Job. 42:2).

What security this is when we remember that God's purposes are designed by One whose nature is love, "who did not spare his own Son but gave him up for us all" (Rom. 8:32).

What could be more encouraging to us as women than to know that the God of love is perfectly in control of all things?

He reigns supreme over our fluctuating female emotions, our husband's moods and decisions, our children's needs, our homes, as well as over the political situations that affect us. God is in control of all things, and He can never make a mistake. "This God—his way is perfect" (Ps. 18:30).

Consider the workings of God, for He is supreme and sovereignly in control over the crooked and the straight of life. "Consider the work of God; who can make straight what he has made crooked? In the day of prosperity be joyful, but in the day of adversity consider; God has made the one as well as the other" (Ecc. 7:13-14).

The "straight" might be viewed as the smooth of life, when it seems that things are fitting together nicely. The "crooked" is when things are still fitting together, but you don't know it!

There is the "crooked" that God causes and the "crooked" that we create for ourselves and God allows. We make mistakes, blunders, messes. We can create disorder, chaos, sadness, and suffering by breaking God's instructions concerning how life is to be lived. Yet He who is in control over all things says concerning the seemingly crooked that He has made, or the crooked we have caused: "All things work together for good to them that love God, to them who are the called according to his purpose" (Rom. 8:28, KJV).

When you despairingly think, "O Lord, bless this mess," Romans 8:28 says He has! Your loving Father, who is in control of everything, has worked even your mistakes into His plans for good!

Discovery I/Sovereignty Described

1. a. Look up the word *sovereign* in a dictionary, and then describe what might be meant by the truth *God is sovereign*. _____

   _____

   _____

    b. Note the similarities between the dictionary definition of *sovereign* and the declaration of 1 Chronicles 29:11-12. What do these verses state about God? __

_____

_____

_____

    c. If you believed and continually remembered this truth, how might it affect your life? _____

_____

_____

2. In each of the following verses, discover different areas in which God's sovereign control of all things is manifested. (As you read each passage, remind yourself that God loves you so much He allowed His Son to die for you.)

    a. Genesis 14:19_____

    b. Deuteronomy 10:14,17_____

    c. 1 Samuel 2:6-8_____

    d. 1 Chronicles 29:11-12_____

    e. 2 Chronicles 20:6_____

    f. Nehemiah 9:6_____

    g. Psalm 47:2-3,7-8 _____

    h. Psalm 50:10-11 _____

    i. Psalm 95:3-5_____

    j. Psalm 115:3 _____

    k. Psalm 135:7 _____

    l. Psalm 145:13 _____

    m. Acts 17:24-26_____

3. Discover the beautiful truth concerning God's sovereignty

illustrated in Matthew 10:29. What does this mean to you in respect to the "small details" of *your* life? _____

_____

_____

4. As you consider the sovereignty of God (review 2 Chronicles 20:6; Job 42:2; and question 2), what do you think could stop God's plans from being carried out in your life?

_____

a. in your husband's life? _____

b. in your children's lives? _____

c. in your home? _____

d. at school? _____

e. in your work situation? _____

f. in the world? _____

Discovery II/The Sovereignty of God in Daily Life

5. a. Rewrite Ecclesiastes 7:13-14 in your own words. ___

_____

_____

b. When things are going "straight" or prosperous in your own life, what do these verses admonish you to do? Give an example to show how you might apply this to your life. _____

_____

_____

_____

c. What are you to do and what is to be the focus of your attention in the day of adversity? Illustrate how you might do this. _____

_____

_____

_____

6. Can you think of a situation from your life that might be thought of as "crooked" that God has made? Realizing that this has come from God, does your perspective of the "crooked" change? _____

_____

_____

_____

7. a. Write down a difficulty which you have brought upon yourself (see introductory section). _____

_____

_____

b. Next, write Romans 8:28 above what you have written and believe God's Word in spite of your emotions concerning the difficulty. Emotions vary; truth cannot.

Discovery III/God's Sovereignty Illustrated in Scripture

8. a. Read Genesis 37 and explain the "crooked" situation in Joseph's life. _____

_____

_____

b. How do you see God's sovereign protection of Joseph demonstrated through this passage? _____

_____

_____

9. What could be called the "straight" of Joseph's early life in Egypt (Gen. 39:1-6)?_____

_____

10. a. Was Joseph responsible for the "crooked" situations in Genesis 39:7-20? _____

_____

b. After reading Genesis 39:21-23, write what you think was Joseph's response to his seeming misfortune. ___

_____

c. What might have been your response?_____

_____

11. God's perfect timing is demonstrated through what interesting aspect of Joseph's prison experience (Gen. 40; 41:1,9-14)? In what ways have you been conscious of God's timing in your life?_____

_____

_____

12. a. God's wise management of all things used Joseph's adverse experiences as a slave and a prisoner to progressively train him for what important task (Gen. 41:25-45)?_____

_____

b. What was Joseph's great testimony to his family of God's control of all things in their life (Gen. 42:1-8; 45:1-11; especially vv. 5-7)? _____

_____

_____

13. What personal applications can you make from this account to your life? _____

_____

_____

Discovery IV/The Sovereignty of God at Work in One Couple's Relationship

14. Read Luke 1:26-38, along with Matthew 1:18-25.
    a. Describe Mary's situation._____

    _____

    _____

    b. Explain Joseph's problem._____

    _____

    c. As Mary considered her situation, upon what did she focus her attention? _____

    _____

    d. How did God sovereignly meet the need of each?__

    _____

    e. Did the "situation" change?_____

    _____

15. a. In what areas of your husband's life and/or your life do you need to trust God to work?_____

    _____

    _____

    b. Reflect on the sovereignty of God as you read Proverbs 3:5-8 and 21:1. Commit those areas to the Lord in prayer.

Discovery V/Realizing the Sovereignty of God in Your Life

16. Behold your God! Practice meditating on God's greatness, majesty, and sovereignty. A growing awareness of the sovereignty of God leads to true stability in life and develops a gentle and quiet spirit within the heart of a woman, which in God's sight is very precious.

4

GOD IS ALL-POWERFUL

Consider the turbulent power of a hurricane, tornado, or atomic explosion, the thundering crash of lightning or a magnificent waterfall.

Now stretch your mind to imagine the fantastic power that restrains the sun from whirling into the earth, that holds the planets in orbit, the moon and stars in their paths. God, as Creator, is the source of all this power, equal to the combined power of all there is!

Yet, Scripture states a most amazing thing. All the power demonstrated in our universe is but a "hiding" or "veiling" of our God's power (Hab. 3:4). Amazing! The magnificent power displayed in the universe conceals more than reveals the limitless power of God. It is but a droplet of His inconceivable power.

God *spoke* and everything that is was made out of *nothing!* You and I must have materials in order to work, but God's plans came into being as He spoke: "for he spoke, and it came to be; he commanded, and it stood forth" (Ps. 33:9). God *said,* "Let there be . . ." and it was, each accomplishment perfect (Gen. 1).

And how does everything He made continue to exist? He ". . . uphold[s] the universe by *his word* of power" (Heb. 1:3). The power of God is incomprehensible; He speaks and it is so!

Since all power belongs to God (Ps. 62:11), there is no such thing as one act being more difficult than another for God. Each of His acts is accomplished through the same effortless power. You see, it is just as easy for God to speak a universe into being as it is for Him to provide you with a needed new coat. It is no more difficult for God to transform a person characterized by hate into a disciple of love than it is for Him to get you through a particularly hectic day effectively and peacefully. There are no bounds to God's effortless power.

But there is more. New life, eternal life, is ours if we "have been born anew, not of perishable seed but of imperishable through the living and abiding *Word of God*" (1 Peter 1:23). By placing your faith in the Word of God concerning the death and resurrection of Jesus Christ, you have become a *new woman* in Christ; the old wife, mother, and "enslaved" woman is *dead;* the new you has come. "Therefore, if any one is in Christ, [she] is a new creation, the old has passed away, behold, the new has come" (2 Cor. 5:17). This is *fact,* but your *experience* of this fact is progressive. And how is this fantastic transformation taking place? Through the *power of His Word!* Imagine the power in the Word of God for you. When believed (and therefore acted upon), it transforms your life. No wonder ". . . the word of God is living and active, sharper than any two-edged sword" (Heb. 4:12).

"For he spoke, and it came to be; he commanded, and it stood forth" (Ps. 33:9). As a Christian woman, you *are* completely new (2 Cor. 5:17).

Another amazing declaration of Scripture is that God all-powerful lives *in you* if you have trusted Christ personally as your Savior. ". . . and we will come to him and make our home with him" (John 14:23); "Christ lives within you . . ." (Rom. 8:10, LB); ". . . and remember that if anyone doesn't have the Spirit of Christ living in him, he is not a Christian at all" (Rom. 8:9, LB).

What does this mean to us as wives and mothers in the practicality of the every day in which we live?

The powerful Word of God declares that the same power that raised Jesus Christ from the dead and seated Him at the right hand of God the Father *is* in us who believe (Eph. 1:19-20). It is this power of God that will enable each of us to be the wife our husband needs in order that he might be what he was created to be. It is God's power in us that enables each of us to be mothers who meet the needs of our children, that they might be raised to hit the "target" for which they were created, "like arrows in the hand of a warrior" (Ps. 127:4). God all-powerful, living in and through you, is the practical explanation of why the Scripture promises:

> I can do all things in him who strengthens [or empowers] me (Phil. 4:13).
>
> As your days, so shall your strength [or power] be (Deut. 33:25).
>
> He who calls you [to a task or into a situation, etc.] is faithful, and he will do it (1 Thess. 5:24).

These promises can be true in your life!

The miraculous truth for you, the Christian woman, is that since God all-powerful lives *within you,* the limitless power of God resides *in you!* The amount of power you need for whatever the situation in which you now or ever will find yourself is already available to you by faith (the activator). ("All things are possible to him who believes.") God will manifest His power through you in the "amount" needed for your situation. "Grace to help in time of need" (Heb. 4:16). "As your days, so shall your strength be" (Deut. 33:25).

Are you in the midst of a situation that, humanly speaking, is beyond you? Perhaps you feel enslaved by a mental attitude of resentment, jealousy, bitterness, anger, hurt, pride, fear, depression, lack of discipline, or a habit which you feel powerless to break. Maybe you face a situation that appears impossible to pass through. Are you struggling on your own when God's power is available to you?

> What is impossible with men is possible with God (Luke 18:27).
>
> Is anything too hard for [God]? (Jer. 32:27).
>
> I can do all things in him who strengthens me (Phil. 4:13).

You can lean on and trust such a One in faith! "Who is like thee, O LORD, . . . who is like unto thee?" (Exod. 15:11). "The Lord is the stronghold of my life" (Ps. 27:1). That we, as women, might be encouraged to choose to place our faith *in* God, that the power of God might become operative in our daily life (Gal. 2:20), we need to mature in our knowledge of God all-powerful—*all-mighty*—*omnipotent*.

Discovery I/God's Power

Depend on the spirit of God to be your teacher as you begin this lesson.

1. Concerning power, the Scriptures declare＿＿＿＿＿＿ (Ps. 62:11).
2. God said of Himself,＿＿＿＿＿＿＿＿＿＿＿ (Gen. 17:1).
3. In Mark 14:62, Jesus Christ uses the word＿＿＿as God's name.
4. What do you discover about God in the following verses?

   a. Deuteronomy 32:39＿＿＿＿＿＿＿＿＿＿

   b. 1 Chronicles 29:12＿＿＿＿＿＿＿＿＿＿

   c. Job 42:2＿＿＿＿＿＿＿＿＿＿＿＿＿

   d. Psalm 135:6＿＿＿＿＿＿＿＿＿＿＿＿

    e. Jeremiah 32:27 _____

    f. Daniel 4:35 _____

    g. Matthew 19:26 _____

5. Whether we acknowledge it or not, the magnificent power of God is being displayed daily to us through:

    a. _____ (Pss. 19:1-4; 36:6b; 66:9)

    b. _____ (Pss. 33:6-9; 89:11-12)

6. Name personal ways these two examples of God's mighty power affect your life. _____

_____

_____

_____

7. The limitless power of God enables Him to accomplish all He wills. Therefore, it is of great comfort to know that:

    a. What God wills is always _____ (Ps. 18:30).

    b. What God wills is always _____ (Pss. 85:12; 106:1).

Discovery II/The Power of God's Word

8. According to the Bible, how was the universe in which our families now live brought into existence (Gen. 1:1-3,6,9,11,14,20,24; Ps. 33:9)? What word is repeated again and again in these verses? _____

_____

_____

9. How is God's creation continuing to exist today (Heb. 1:3)?_____

_____

10. Read John 1:1-4,14. Who is referred to as the Word in these verses? _____

11. During His earthly ministry, Jesus Christ demonstrated His power.

a. over_____(Matt. 8:3).

b. over _____ (Luke 5:18-25).

c. over _____ (Luke 8:22-24).

d. over _____ (Luke 8:27-33).

e. over _____(John 11:41-45).

12. a. List what things Colossians 1:15-17 declares of Jesus Christ. _____
_____

b. What may be concluded concerning Jesus Christ? (Besides the verses above, consider John 10:30 and Psalm 62:11).

Discovery III/Power to Transform

Since God is all-powerful, He can transform *even you.*

13. a. Meditate on the following two basic concepts from questions 4 and 7:

   1) God has all power, "No one can hinder His plans"; and

   2) His will is always best.

b. Now relate this knowledge to a difficult or "impossible" problem you are now in. Think about your situation from this divine viewpoint.

c. List some of your new conclusions. _____
_____
_____
_____

d. Scripture describes the process you are now doing as

_____(Rom. 12:2).

e. Name the result in your life if you continue in this process according to Romans 12:2. Put in your own words what this "result" means. (A dictionary may help you to better understand the word.)_____

_____

_____

Discovery IV/The Power of God Illustrated

The following historical accounts are of two men empowered for unique tasks. In both men, God Himself was the object of their faith.

14. Read 1 Samuel 17:1-31 to get the background to the event. Describe the sharp contrast between David on the one hand and his brothers and countrymen on the other.

_____

_____

_____

15. a. David also stands in contrast to Saul. On what basis does Saul feel that David is unprepared to fight Goliath (1 Sam. 17:33)?_____

_____

 b. Though Saul's men have been trained, what is their response to a difficult situation (17:24)?_____

_____

 c. Read 1 Samuel 17:34-40. How and by whom has David been trained?_____

_____

_____

 d. What is the result of this type of training (17:32,36-37)?

_____

_____

_____

e. As David reasons with Saul, what does he demonstrate that he knows about God (17:37)? _____

_____

f. Does David only "talk" about God, or does he believe in God's power? How do you know? (17:37,40) ____

_____

_____

g. When you say, "God is all-powerful and all-loving," and then worry and become anxious, what does that mean?_____

_____

_____

16. a. Who does David say is empowering his arm? Who is really facing Goliath (1 Sam. 17:45-46)? _____

_____

b. As God empowered David, what is His promise to you found in Isaiah 41:10?_____

_____

_____

17. The prophet Elijah prayed that it would not rain for three years, and it didn't. Then at the end of the three years, Elijah prayed for rain. While the prophet prayed, clouds began appearing on the horizon.

a. In order for Elijah, the representative of God, to be the one to proclaim God's miracle of rain to the people, what amazing feat did he have to perform (1 Kings 18:44-46)?_____

_____

_____

b. What phrase explains how Elijah was able to do this?

_____

   c. Do you think this feat was difficult for God (Jer. 32:17)?

_____

Discovery V/God's Power in You

18. What amazing things has God's power accomplished for you (Col. 1:12-14)? _____

_____

_____

19. a. In what is Paul placing confidence as he prays (Col. 1:11) for the Colossian believers (Eph. 3:20)? _____

_____

   b. In Colossians 1:11, Paul states that the Colossians must have God's power for _____ and _____ with _____.

20. For what is God's power needed in Isaiah 40:29-31 and 41:10? _____

_____

_____

Do you feel the need for God's power in any of the areas mentioned in questions 19 and 20? Which in particular?

_____

_____

21. a. As a Christian woman, what is the basis for you to be able to face without fear every situation of life (Ps. 27:1)? _____

_____

   b. This power of God becomes experiential in your life as you (John 15:17; 16:24; Heb. 11:6; 1 John 5:14-15):

_____

_____

5

GOD IS GOOD

Did you know that all the *good* things you ever received, saw, felt, heard, tasted, or smelled came from the living God? The Scriptures reveal that "every good endowment and perfect gift is from above, coming down from the Father of lights . . ." (James 1:17).

When the Scripture proclaims, "God is good" (Nahum 1:7; Pss. 25:8; 86:5; 119:69), the absolute declaration being made is that God is the source of *all* goodness in the universe. Therefore, *good cannot be found apart from God.*

The psalmist states concerning man living apart from God that ". . . there is none that does good" (Ps. 14:1-3). You cannot be surprised when you turn from God and from following His good commands that you do not find good. You never will find good apart from God and His ways!

Because God is absolute good, He has never done nor can He ever do one thing to you that is not good. God also cannot change (see "God Is Immutable"), and so has never been more or less good to you than He is right now. God is being as good to you this minute as when He died that you might have life! Because He possesses unlimited power and is perfectly in control of all things, God may always accomplish His totally wise and good plans for you. This is why "all things work together for good to them that love God . . ." (Rom. 8:28, KJV). Realizing this truth leads to peaceful stability in our life as well as dissolving our fears.

Consider the goodness of God and be encouraged in the daily events of your life. Though you may not understand God's ways because of your limited perspective of what is actually taking place around you, you may have total confidence that God's actions toward you are always for your good; ". . . the LORD will give what is good," for "this God—his way is perfect" (Pss. 85:12; 18:30).

Discovery I/The Attribute Set Forth

1. a. Nahum 1:7 sets forth what truth concerning the nature of God? (Living daily in the light of this great truth will powerfully affect our lives as women.) _____

   _____

   b. How might the fact that God is good be a "stronghold" to you in the day of trouble? _____

   _____

   _____

2. a. Because God is good, what will He do (Ps. 25:8-9)?

   _____

   b. God will accomplish this through His will, which can be described as_____
   (Rom. 12:2), and His commands, which are _____,
   _____, and _____(Rom. 7:12).

3. What then should you realize as you discover the various commands of God revealed in the Scripture? (A review of

questions 1 and 2, along with Deuteronomy 5:29 and 6:24, will help you answer). _____

_____

_____

4. Explain *in your own words* the amazing truth James 1:17 reveals concerning every good thing from the smallest to the greatest that has ever happened to you. _____

_____

_____

Discovery II/God's Goodness Demonstrated in the World

5. a. State God's opinion of His creation after He had brought it into existence by the word of His power (Gen. 1:31)._____

_____

   b. Explain the tragic contrast between Genesis 1:31 and 6:5-6 in light of Genesis 2:15-17 and 3:1-8._____

_____

_____

6. In spite of all the events recorded in Genesis 3, what is still true according to Psalm 33:5? (KJV preferred here). ____

_____

_____

7. a. Who are the recipients of the goodness of God (Matt. 5:43-45)?_____

_____

   b. How can the Christian be like God (Matt. 5:44-48)?

_____

c. How might the command to "love your enemies" free you and therefore be for your own good? _____

_____

_____

8. Indicate from the following passages specific evidences of the daily goodness of the Lord to all. Personally apply at least two of these verses to your own life.

a. Genesis 8:21-22 _____

b. Psalm 36:6b (KJV preferred) _____

c. Psalm 145:9,15-16 _____

d. Matthew 6:26-30 _____

e. Acts 14:17 _____

9. Explain the supreme demonstration of God's goodness to you and all mankind as revealed in Romans 5:6-8 and Galatians 4:4-6. _____

_____

_____

_____

Discovery III/The Goodness of God Expressed to the Believer

10. God's goodness is illustrated in His blessings to the believer in Jesus Christ. List the blessings expressed in the following verses and write your name into each. *Example:* John 1:12 *God has given power to* Susan *to become the child of God.*

a. John 1:12 (cf. 1 John 3:1; Eph. 1:5) _____

_____

b. Romans 8:28 _____

_____

c. Romans 8:32 _____

_____

d. Ephesians 1:3-6 _____

_____

e. Ephesians 1:7-8 _____

_____

f. Ephesians 1:13 _____

_____

g. 2 Peter 1:3-4 _____

_____

11. As you reflect on your discoveries of God's goodness to you, what do Psalms 34:8 and 107:1,8 call on you to do? Have you done this? _____

_____

_____

12. a. According to Romans 2:4, what is to be a result of the goodness of God in your life? Can you give an example from your own experience? _____

_____

_____

b. What other specific action does the goodness and kindness of God encourage in us (Ps. 36:7)? _____

_____

Discovery IV/God's Goodness Expressed Through the Believer

13. Discover a significant reason for a Christian woman's existence on this earth according to Psalm 34:14; Ephesians 2:10; Colossians 1:10; and Titus 3:8. How might the main command seen in these verses be for your own

good? In what way does this command relate to God's general purpose for believers found in Romans 8:29?__

_____

_____

_____

14. What is the important adornment for women in the sight of God? (1 Tim. 2:9-10) How does this truth challenge you in respect to rearing a daughter? _____

_____

_____

_____

15. Since this womanly adornment is so precious in the sight of God, it is important to discover biblical examples of good works. List some examples of good works from the following:

   a. Psalm 133:1 _____

   b. Proverbs 12:25 _____

   c. Micah 6:8 _____

   d. Matthew 5:44-45 _____

   e. Romans 12:9-21_____

   _____

   _____

   _____

   _____

   f. 1 Thessalonians 5:15-21 _____

   _____

   g. 1 Timothy 2:1-3 _____

   _____

h. Titus 2:4-5 _____

_____

i. Titus 3:1-2 _____

_____

16. When you as a wife and mother desire to do good for your family, who has initiated that motivation within you according to Philippians 2:13? _____

_____

17. Use Romans 7:18-19,24-25; 2 Corinthians 9:8; 1 Thessalonians 5:24; and 2 Peter 1:3 to explain what God has done to enable you to accomplish good. (These verses are particularly good to reflect on when you feel frustrated in attempts to do good.) _____

_____

_____

_____

18. What will be the end results of your good works:

a. upon others (1 Peter 2:12)? _____

b. upon yourself (Deut. 6:24)? _____

Realize *now* that as a Christian woman, the living God, the source of all goodness, is alive within you! As you depend on Him, His goodness will pour out through you to your family and to others. "God is able to provide you with every blessing in abundance, so that you may always have enough of everything and may provide in abundance for every good work" (2 Cor. 9:8).

6

GOD IS OMNISCIENT

You have just explained to your husband how you feel, and he stares at you with a blank women-have-got-to-be-God's-strangest-creation look. You think, *Am I an island? Doesn't anybody know or understand what I am saying?*

God's Word answers, "I know everything you think—every thought that comes into your minds" (Ezek. 11:5, LB). "You [Lord] know my every thought" (Ps. 139:2, LB).

How wonderful! God knows; Someone understands what we are thinking!

You're "blue" or frustrated. You have a need, but you don't know what it is.

God's Word encourages, "My God will supply every need of yours" (Phil. 4:19). How can God do this? He *knows* your needs.

You're in anguish, overwhelmed by grief—no one can feel the pain of your sorrow; you reason, "Yes, Lord, You know the facts; You know even what I'm thinking; but do You know how I *feel?*"

"For we have not a high priest who is unable to sympathize with our weaknesses, but one who in every respect has been tempted as we are, yet without sin. Let us then with confidence draw near to the throne of grace, that we may receive mercy and find grace to help in time of need" (Heb. 4:15-16).

The scriptural truth on which these biblical answers are based is the fact that God *knows everything*. God always knew everything and, therefore, never had to learn anything! "Who has directed the Spirit of the LORD or as his counselor has instructed him?" (Isa. 40:13).

What does the phrase "God knows everything" mean? We seem to need a picture for our minds in order to begin to. glimpse this incomprehensible aspect of God's character. For illustration, take the idea of "movement" and consider this aspect of experience in light of God's omniscience. "Known [completely] unto God are all his works from the beginning of the world" (Acts 15:18, KJV). A total knowledge of all His works would mean that God knows every wing flutter of each fly, bee, or bird at this very moment. Each gentle sway of grass is known by God. Every human step, jerk of the head, and unconscious finger tapping is perceived by God (Ps. 139:1-3). Our God knows the tiniest movement that ever occurred or will occur, and this knowledge is but the smallest fraction of His omniscience!

Another amazing thing about God's omniscience is that not only does He know the minutest detail of the past, present, and future, but He also knows all the possibilities; He knows the "what ifs" (1 John 3:20; Matt. 11:21-24)! Have you ever wondered, "What if it had all happened another way?" God knows exactly what would have happened! How obvious that we should seek counsel and direction from our God who alone perceives the whole picture. "Wait for the LORD. . . . I will instruct you and teach you the way you should go") Pss. 27:14; 32:8).

God knows *everything* about you. Yet, knowing every motive, every secret sin, He still loves you. "Thou hast set our iniquities before thee, our secret sins in the light of thy countenance" (Ps. 90:8). "While we were yet sinners Christ died for us" (Rom. 5:8).

He loves you! What relief knowing you do not have to be something you're not; you're loved even as you are. No one can sneak up to God and reveal something that will cause Him to turn His love from you. No weakness of character is going to float to the surface and suddenly surprise God, causing His love for you to diminish. Though He knows everything about you there is to know, you are of such unestimable value to God that He died so He could have a personal relationship with you for eternity!

He *knows* each detail of the situation in which you now live. "You know when I sit or stand. . . . Every moment, you know where I am" (Ps. 139:2-3).

No one else may know about or understand your present situation, but God does completely. Not only does He know, but He knows your limit, how much you can take: "For he knows our frame; he remembers that we are dust" (Ps. 103:14).

How comforting to realize that because God knows our frame, He knows what we will need in the future as well as at the present moment. His knowledge of our future needs is the basis for His promise, "Before they call I will answer, while they are yet speaking I will hear" (Isa. 65:24). How can God answer a request not yet asked? He knew what your request would be before you asked.

God's knowledge encompasses past, present, and future all at the same time; from the rise and fall of nations to the path of an ant, each detail is known by Him. Since God alone knows the future, *only He* can predict it. Each biblical prophecy that has been fulfilled has been fulfilled in every detail, and just so will all future biblical prophecies be fulfilled.

Only the prophets of God are right 100 percent of the time!

Because He alone knows the future, only God can prepare you for yours, and He has promised to do just that: "I will instruct you and teach you the way you should go; I will counsel you with my eye upon you" (Ps. 32:8). His instruction is in His Word to illumine our way: "Thy word is a lamp to my feet and a light to my path" (Ps. 119:105).

Discovery I/God Is All-Knowing

1. Scripture reveals specifics to enable finite man to begin to grasp the infinite concept that God knows everything! In the following verses, discover some of these and personalize your answers:

   a. Job 23:10_____

   b. Psalm 103:14 _____

   c. Psalm 139:2-4_____

   d. Psalm 147:5 _____

   e. Ezekiel 11:5 _____

   f. Daniel 2:22_____

   g. Acts 15:18 (KJV)_____

   h. Hebrews 4:13_____

2. "Know (*completely*, in every detail) unto God are all his works from the beginning" (Acts 15:18, KJV). How do Psalm 50:11 and Matthew 10:30 give us a glimpse into this "complete" knowledge? _____

   _____

   _____

3. a. The omniscience and goodness of God enables Him to make judgments that are always _____ (Jer. 11:20) because He knows all the facts and aspects involved and He always does good.

b. What should this mean to you when you read in Scripture about God's judgments? _____

_____

_____

4. a. As you consider your discoveries, do you think God ever wonders about anything? Does God need to ask questions or discover facts? Why or why not?_____

_____

_____

b. From your understanding of God's omniscience, how might you view the decisions God has made concerning the direction of your life?_____

_____

_____

Discovery II/God's Knowledge and the Predictions of the Future

The Scriptures declare that only God can know the future (Isa. 41:22-24; 44:6-8). God set up a specific test so that people might be certain whether or not a prophet was from God. The conditions of the test were simple and clear: if a prophet met the test perfectly, he was of God; if he failed in any area, he was not from God.

5. a. Discover God's prophet test in Deuteronomy 18:18-22 and summarize it briefly._____

_____

_____

b. How would you evaluate the "religious" psychics of today in light of God's test? _____

_____

_____

6. The episode recorded in 1 Samuel 23:8-14 reveals two specific aspects of God's knowledge of the future. Discover these. (Refer back to introductory section.)_____

_____

_____

7. a. Can you think of specific ways God prepared you in the past for the "future" He knew you would be experiencing today? List these._____

_____

_____

_____

  b. How can you "be prepared" for your future? _____

_____

_____

_____

Discovery III/Jesus Christ Is Omniscient

8. What person is revealed in John 21:17 as knowing everything?_____

9. Note how the following biblical examples illustrate the truth of John 21:17:
   a. Who knows completely the incomprehensible God, our Father (Matt. 11:27; 1 Cor. 2:10-13)? _____

_____

   b. What does the account of Jesus' healing of the man with the withered hand reveal that Jesus knew about the observers of this event (Luke 6:6-11; cf. Ezek. 11:5)?_____

_____

_____

    c. In what two ways do the denunciations of Jesus Christ against the New Testament cities of Chorazin and Bethsaida (Matt. 11:21-24) show that Jesus Christ is all-knowing? (Chorazin and Bethsaida were destroyed by the fourth century A.D.) _____

_____

_____

    d. How do you think Jesus could accurately tell the woman at the well about her "husbands" (John 4:16-19)?_____

_____

_____

    e. John 6:64 declares that Jesus knew_____

_____

10. Since God is all-knowing, what are the Scriptures proclaiming concerning Jesus Christ?_____

_____

Discovery IV/God's Total Knowledge of You

11. a. What does 1 Chronicles 28:9 specifically declare that God knows *about you?*_____

_____

    b. In what way is this an encouragement to you this week?_____

_____

_____

12. a. Read Psalm 139 and make a list of all the things God knows about you._____

_____

_____

b. As you meditate on Psalm 139:13-15, do you think God made a mistake when He "knit" *you* together in your mother's womb? (Use what you know of the character of God to help you answer.) _____

_____

_____

c. How might viewing yourself in the light of this truth affect your self-concept? _____

_____

_____

13. a. In what ways do Psalms 56:8 and 142:3 reveal that God is specifically aware of your secret struggles and sorrows? _____

_____

_____

b. In the light of this truth, consider a recent struggle or sorrow you have experienced. What does it mean to you to realize God cared so intimately about your turmoil? _____

_____

_____

14. a. Rewrite Hebrews 4:13 in personal words which include your own name. _____

_____

_____

b. God, being all-knowing, is able to _____

_____

(Ps. 90:8; Jer. 2:22; Hos. 7:2).

c. However, when you believe in the truth found in Romans 5:8, what does God say He will do for you (Ps. 103:10-12; Isa. 43:25)?_____

_____

d. Has God done this for you? How do you know? ____

_____

15. a. Relate some of your discoveries from this lesson to the great promise of Philippians 4:19._____

_____

_____

b. List some of your present needs. _____

_____

_____

c. Remembering that God knows you completely, write Philippians 4:19 under your list. What does this mean?

_____

_____

Discovery V/The Knowledge of God in the Believer

16. a. According to Colossians 2:2-3, where is the source of true knowledge and wisdom to be found?_____

_____

b. As a Christian woman, what do you possess?_____

_____

_____

17. In light of this study, how is it possible for you to be used to meet
    a. your husband's needs?_____

    _____

    _____

    b. your child's needs?_____

    _____

    _____

    c. your friends' needs? _____

    _____

    _____

7

GOD IS ALL-WISE

Knowledge is the amount of information one possesses.
Wisdom is the use of that information.
Biblical wisdom is knowledge digested and applied correctly to a given situation for the best results.

"Blessed be the name of God forever and ever, for he alone has all wisdom" (Dan. 2:20, LB). God is all-wise; that is, He has an unlimited ability to apply correctly His all-encompassing knowledge. God is good and thus can produce only good. Therefore, God's knowledge applied (wisdom) will always result in the best possible good.

Because God cannot sacrifice one attribute for another, each decision of the almighty God is as loving as it is wise and good. Because of God's knowledge, wisdom, and loving goodness, there can be no way to improve upon God's ways; they are perfect. "This God—his way is perfect" (Ps. 18:30). God can never make a mistake. What security for those who lean not on their own understanding, but on the wisdom of God alone.

As a human being, you are more or less limited to an ant's-eye view of your life situations. In contrast to this, God knows exactly what He is allowing in your life. He sees the total picture of your circumstances. He has chosen for you the best direction to achieve His transforming and loving purposes in you and in the flow of history.

Consider how an all-wise God led the men and women of the Bible through a great variety of circumstances specifically chosen to teach them the liberating principles of faith in Him alone. While His personal work was taking place in their lives, God was accomplishing His overall purpose in history through the same men and women.

Just so, God is carefully leading you through life situations wisely designed to develop within you a new nature after the likeness of His own. God's method of developing this new nature is by teaching you how to respond in reliance on Him in daily life situations. Realizing that the situation you are facing has been designed by God in loving wisdom encourages your faith response.

"I will instruct you and teach you the way you should go; I will counsel you with my eye upon you; . . . [that you might] be conformed to the image of [Jesus Christ]" (Ps. 32:8; Rom. 8:29).

You will never fully understand God's ways or be able to offer concrete reasons for all His acts "For my thoughts are not your thoughts, neither are your ways my ways, says the LORD" (Isa. 55:8). But you can *know* by a faith-decision on the basis of His *all-wise* character that His ways are perfect no matter how bad things look or how you "feel" about them. "And I will lead the blind in a way that they know not, in paths that they have not known I will guide them. I will turn the darkness before them into light, the rough places into level ground. These are the things I will do, and I will not forsake them" (Isa. 42:16).

Discovery I/The Attribute Discovered

1. a. What is the difference between one who possesses knowledge and one who demonstrates wisdom? ___

   _____

   _____

   b. Do you think knowledge is an end in itself? Why or why not? _____

   _____

   _____

   c. Can you have wisdom without knowledge? Explain.

   _____

   _____

   _____

2. Discover what the Scriptures declare about God in Isaiah 28:29, Daniel 2:20-22; and Romans 16:27. _____

   _____

   _____

   _____

3. a. On the basis of the truth found in the verses above, from whom should you first seek counsel in any situation? _____

   _____

   b. Has this been the habit of your life? _____

   _____

4. Is it possible for God to act in wisdom in your life apart from His other characteristics? Why is this important for you to remember? _____

   _____

   _____

5. Name the distinguishing characteristics James 3:17 gives to describe the wisdom of God. _____

_____

_____

6. What do you think is a basis for the promise God makes in Psalm 32:8? _____

_____

Discovery II/Biblical Illustration of God's Wise Counsel

7. Read 2 Chronicles 20:1-13.
   a. Briefly summarize the problem facing the people of God. _____

   _____

   _____

   b. What was the king's (and most likely the people's) initial reaction to their predicament?_____

   _____

   c. What was the king's first concrete step in dealing with the problem? Is this usually your first step in the midst of difficulties? _____

   _____

   _____

   d. In light of the following Scriptures, why do you think this was the best first step he could have taken: Proverbs 1:7; Isaiah 26:3-4; 31:1,3)?_____

   _____

   _____

   e. At the beginning of Jehoshaphat's prayer before the Lord, of what truths concerning God does the king remind himself and all the people?_____

   _____

f. Why do you think it might be good for you to praise the Lord as you bring.a difficult problem to Him in prayer?

_____

_____

g. What phrases in this prayer lead you to believe the heart attitude of the king was one of:
   1) humility before the Lord? _____

   _____

   _____

   2) dependence on the Lord? _____

   _____

   _____

8. Read 2 Chronicles 20:13-30.
   a. What was God's specific counsel to the people through His spokesman Jahaziel? _____

   _____

   _____

   b. Do you think this counsel would have seemed a strange battle plan from the world's perspective? (See Isa. 55:8.) Explain _____

   _____

   c. According to the passage, to whom did this battle belong? _____

   d. Was God's counsel heeded? What was the result?

   _____

   _____

   e. What effect did trust placed in God have on the countries surrounding Jerusalem? _____

   _____

9. What personal lessons has the Holy Spirit taught you as you studied this illustration of what happens when God's wisdom is heeded? _____

_____

_____

_____

_____

Discovery III/The Discovery of God's Wisdom in You

10. a. Where is the source of true wisdom found (Col. 2:2-3)?

_____

   b. In light of Colossians 2:2-3 and 1 Corinthians 2:14-16, do you think it would be possible for one who despises Jesus Christ to be truly wise? _____

_____

11. a. As a woman who believes in Jesus Christ as Savior, what amazing yet practical truth is revealed to you in 1 Corinthians 2:16 and James 1:5?_____

_____

   b. What prerequisite does James 1:5 give for your receiving wisdom? _____

_____

   c. In what way does your study of the Word of God prepare you to receive wisdom from God? (Review the definition of wisdom found in the introductory section.)_____

_____

_____

12. The woman of Proverbs 31:10-31 is described as one who "opens her mouth with wisdom" (v. 26).
    a. What do you think is meant by this statement? Could this statement be applied to you? Why or why not?

    _____

    _____

    b. Can you give an example of how you applied your knowledge of God to a given situation? What was the result?_____

    _____

    _____

13. a. To whom does the revealed knowledge and wisdom of God belong (Deut. 29:29)? (The pronoun *us* in the verse refers by application to believers in Jesus Christ.)

    _____

    b. We desire our children to have wisdom. In light of this desire, what do Deuteronomy 29:29 and 6:6-9 suggest to you concerning your children? _____

    _____

    _____

Discovery IV/The Result of the Wisdom of God in a Woman's Life

14. According to Proverbs 1:20-32, what will be the results in a life when God's knowledge and wisdom are shunned?

    _____

    _____

_____

_____

15. In great contrast to Proverbs 1:20-32, what is the result in your life when you respond to God's wisdom (Prov. 1:33)?

_____

_____

16. a. List what Proverbs 4:6-12 promises will accompany the development of true wisdom in your life. _____

_____

_____

_____

_____

_____

_____

b. In what way could these "results" affect
   1) your personal life? _____

   _____

   _____

   2) your marriage? _____

   _____

   _____

Discovery V/All Wisdom Reserved for God

17. On earth, will *you* ever understand everything about God and His ways? Why or why not? (See 1 Cor. 13:9 and Deut. 29:29; Isa. 55:8-9) _____

_____

_____

18. Believers will not always be able to know "why" something happened to them. However, as a believer in Jesus Christ, what can you know for certain (Rom. 8:28)?

_____

_____

8

GOD IS OMNIPRESENT

Right this moment you are surrounded by the presence of God. As you ride to the store or arrive at the office, you continue to be enveloped by His presence, for God is everywhere. You cannot go where God is not (Ps. 139:7-12)!

This presence is not the presence of a part of God, for God is not divided, diffused, or spread throughout the entire universe like minerals in the ground; nor is He a great giant with one part here, another there. God has no "parts"; He is one! *All that God is, is totally present everywhere.* Everywhere we go, we are surrounded by God. We are, therefore, always in the presence of God, whether in the difficult moments of life or in the good, seemingly more "spiritual," times.

The word *presence* literally means "face." The concept of *presence* is that of facing or looking at a person eye-to-eye. Psalm 139:7 states the omnipresence of God this way: "Whither shall I go from thy Spirit? Or whither shall I flee from thy presence?" In other words, *everything* God is, is continually facing or being directed toward you! "Thou God seest me" (Gen. 16:13, KJV). No wonder He can promise, "I will counsel you with my *eye* upon you" (Ps. 32:8).

Jesus said, "I will never fail you nor forsake you" (Heb. 13:5) and "Lo I am with you always" (Matt. 28:20). How could He ever leave you? God's very nature is that of being always present! Awareness by faith (not necessarily feeling) of this truth produces a calm assurance and peace. God is closer than breath, than eyelids and fingernails. And for the Christian woman, all of God is literally inside her in a most unique way through the Holy Spirit.

God fills space with His whole being: "Do I not fill heaven and earth? says the LORD" (Jer. 23:24). "Space" conditions our thoughts. For example, if you are now inside your home, we know that you are not also at the store. But space limitations in no way affect God, for He is spirit (John 4:24). God also exists *outside* of space and is not subject to space limitations. "Heaven and the highest heaven cannot contain thee" (1 Kings 8:27). God is not contained in space (like our spirit is by our body while we live on earth, like an embryo is in the womb). It is just the opposite; it is "space" that is *inside God!* "*In him* we live and move and have our being" (Acts 17:28). "*In him* all things hold together" (Col. 1:17).

Applying this thrilling truth to the concept of God's love in the everyday life of the believer, Paul says:

> Who shall separate us from the love of Christ? Shall tribulation, or distress, or persecution, or famine, or nakedness, or peril, or sword? . . . For I am sure that neither death, nor life, nor angels, nor principalities, nor things present, nor things to come, nor powers, nor height, nor depth, nor anything else in all creation, will be able to separate us from the love of God in Christ Jesus our Lord (Rom. 8:35,38-39).

What security! What a source of encouragement is the truth that God is everywhere. In every place, you, as a Christian, have a Guide, a Protector, a Father, a Friend; ready and effectual aid is always available to you. God is your ready Guide: "I will counsel you with my eye upon you. . . . There thy hand shall lead me" (Pss. 32:8; 139:10). "Your right hand shall hold me" (Ps. 139:10).

Becoming aware of the fact that God is always with you, you need never fear darkness or circumstances. The psalmist said, "Surely the darkness shall cover me." But remembering God's omnipresence, he joyously declares, "But the night shineth as the day [to God]" (Ps. 139:11-12, KJV).

The psalmist concludes, "In thy presence there *is* fulness of joy" (Ps. 16:11). Since we are always in the presence of God, we have the potential for fullness of joy. Oh, that we might realize by faith God's continual presence!

Discovery I/The Scriptures Teach the Omnipresence of God

1. The amazing truth that we are continually in the presence of God is communicated in a variety of ways in the Bible. How does each of the following verses reveal the truth that God is always present?

   a. 1 Kings 8:27 _____

   b. Psalm 139:7-10 _____

   c. Acts 17:27-28 _____

   d. Ephesians 4:6 _____

2. What do you think is meant by "heaven and the highest heaven cannot contain thee" (1 Kings 8:27)? _____

   _____

   _____

3. The literal meaning of the word *presence* is _____. (See the introductory section.) How might this meaning help you to better understand God's omnipresence when you are in a fearful situation? _____

_____

_____

4. a. With the omnipresence of God as his basis, what could the psalmist declare concerning his daily life (Ps. 139:5-6)? _____

   _____

   _____

   b. This week at least once a day, reflect on this truth. Write out any insights that come to you during this reflection.

5. What impossible thing did Jonah think he could do (Jonah 1:1-3)? Compare Psalm 139:7-10. _____

   _____

   _____

6. Often events in our lives teach us truths concerning the character of God. What did Jonah finally realize about God, and what did it take to teach him this truth (Jonah 1:4-7; 2:1-9 [Jonah's testimony])? _____

   _____

   _____

   _____

7. a. What does Jonah declare he finally remembered at the point his "soul fainted within" him (2:7)? _____

   _____

   b. What did the Lord do in answer to Jonah's prayer (2:10)? _____

   _____

8. Rewrite Acts 17:28 in your own words, placing yourself into the verse. _____

   _____

9. a. How do the following passages "picture" God to illustrate the immensity of the Almighty?
   1) Isaiah 40:12,15,22 _____

   _____

   _____

   2) Isaiah 66:1 _____

   _____

   _____

   b. Why do you think the biblical writers used such "pictures" of God? _____

   _____

   _____

   c. In contrast to human form, in reality God is _____
   _____ (John 4:24).

Discovery II/The Omnipresence of God Made Temporarily Visible

10. a. According to the account in Daniel 3:1-15, what was being required of the Jewish exiles Shadrach, Meshach, and Abednego? _____

    _____

    _____

   b. What had God commanded in His Word that would enable the three young men to know God's will in this matter (Deut. 5:7-9)? _____

   _____

   _____

11. What was the response of these men to their difficult situation, and what do you think was the basis for their

decision (Dan. 3:16-18)? _____

_____

_____

12. What does the passage reveal that these men knew about God that enabled them to place determined faith in Him (3:16-18)? _____

_____

13. State the "immediate" result of their godly stand (3:19-23) that God allowed in order to bring glory to His name.

_____

14. a. Describe the miraculous event which then took place before the eyes of King Nebuchadnezzar (3:24-25).

_____

_____

   b. Is the presence of God normally visible to human eyes (1 Tim. 1:17)? _____

   c. On the basis of 1 Timothy 1:17, what was exceptional about the event in the fiery furnace?_____

_____

_____

15. List three aspects of the glorious end result of the stand of these men who made their decision in light of God's Word (3:26-30). _____

_____

_____

_____

Can you give an illustration of a time you chose to follow God's specific commands and the immediate effect appeared negative, but later you became aware of blessing because God was with you? _____

_____

_____

_____

Discovery III/Paul's Testimony

16. a. Compare the Old Testament event found in Daniel 3
with Paul's testimony in 2 Timothy 4:16-18._____

_____

_____

_____

b. How do these two accounts illustrate the certainty of
Jesus' promise in Matthew 28:20?_____

_____

_____

c. Relate this same promise to a present issue in your own
life. _____

_____

_____

Discovery IV/Practicing the Presence of God

17. a. Try to share the fact that God is always present with
one or all of your children in a way they can understand. (Do the same with a friend's child if you are not a
mother.) What was their response? _____

_____

_____

_____

   b. Why do you think it is important for children to become aware of this fact that God is always with them?

   _____

18. How might you specifically apply your new knowledge of the omnipresence of God to your life? (Remember faith in God is based on *facts* concerning God, *not feeling*.) _____

   _____

   _____

19. Memorize Psalm 139:5,7 in order to reflect on the omnipresence of God.

9

GOD IS IMMUTABLE

"Help! Stop the world! I want to get off for a moment. Everything is changing so fast, I need to get my bearings."

Your security rested in familiar surroundings and now a family move has placed you in a totally unfamiliar setting. Help! Your security lay in a smooth, quiet life style and now things are hectic, in flux and turmoil. Help! Your security was placed in your husband's paycheck and now your husband has lost his job. Help! Your security rested in a friend and now she's gone. Help!

In the midst of a world in constant change, how can we stabilize? To whom can we turn when all seems like the grass that withers? Where lies real *security?*

"I the Lord do not change" (Mal. 3:6).

But *everything* must change, we argue. Flowers bud, bloom, wilt; ugly caterpillars become beautiful butterflies, which finally flutter no more; hillsides erode; shiny new tools rust; new cloth frays with age; houses crumble; babies change into children, children to teen-agers, to adults, to senior citizens; beauty queens get wrinkles.

"I the Lord do not change!"

Everything in our world seems to be in continual flux. However, it is this very issue of change that brings into sharper focus the contrast between the changing world and its changeless Creator. Just as the continual change and turbulance of pounding waves against a majestic rock causes us to more fully appreciate the stability of the rock, so change highlights the security to be found in the unwavering, unchangeable Rock that is our God. In experiencing change, we learn to appreciate the Changeless One.

The God of the Scriptures is not progressing, developing, growing, getting better or worse, for He is and has always been absolute perfection, the "same yesterday and today and for ever" (Heb. 13:8). Therefore, God can state His name as: "I AM WHO I AM" (Exod. 3:14).

"All that He is today, He has ever been and ever will be. God has always been perfect in everything and therefore cannot become more" (A. W. Pink).

Since God is the only one who can never change, our true and lasting security lies only in Him and in His ways. Because man is "unstable as water" (Gen. 49:4), our loving, immutable Father warns us not to put our trust "in princes, in a son of man, in whom there is no help" (Ps. 146:3). God alone can be trusted, for nothing can influence or change Him from His nature of total goodness. God is the only truly stable object of faith for man. All else may change around us, but as Christian women, we may live secure as we remember that it is in the Changeless One "we live and move and have our being" (Acts. 17:28).

Though a husband's or friend's attitude toward us may fluctuate, God's attitude is the same as when He, in love, died for us. We never need to worry whether we will find God's attitude receptive when we humbly come to Him after really "blowing it." God does not get into moods or lose His affections: "I have loved you with an everlasting love" (Jer. 31:3). His love does not change—what security!

The changelessness of God affects all His other attributes; nothing about God can ever change. God will always possess knowledge of everything and the ability to make perfect use of His knowledge of all issues involved through His wisdom. Furthermore, His power to carry out His righteous decisions will never lessen. God never changes His mind about anything.* It would be impossible for something "new" to arise to cause God not to stand behind His Word. Therefore, the Scriptures proclaim: "For ever, O LORD, thy word is firmly fixed in the heavens" (Ps. 119:89). "The counsel of the LORD stands for ever, the thoughts of his heart to all generations" (Ps. 33:11). As God cannot change, neither can His purposes and promises, which must therefore be fulfilled. He must be perfectly faithful to promises such as: "Train up a child in the way he should go, and when he is old he will not depart from it" (Prov. 22:6).

"I can do all things in him [Christ] who strengthens me" (Phil. 4:13). What security! And realizing our security in Him, we are free to be a helpmate to our husband, following his leadership whether weak or strong. Knowing security in Christ, we are free to humble ourselves before our children and minister to their real needs. (An insecure mother tends to minister to her child's wants for fear of rejection or a defiance she would

---

*In frequent places in Scripture (Gen. 6:6 and Jonah 3:9,10, for example), it is said that "God repented." This is a human expression which has its meaning in the fact that God acts consistently toward humankind in regard to sin. As long as men are unrepentant, God must pronounce judgment; when they repent, as did the Ninevites, God must act mercifully. In His foreknowledge, God knew what would happen and was not taken by surprise, as if He had to go back on His word.

Note that in the Hebrew there are two words translated *repent:* one properly means "to turn back, to change direction"; the other means "to be sorry, to grieve."

not be able to handle, or out of a selfish love which seeks quick, stop-gap "tranquilizers.") We long to be consistent as wives and mothers, and the Scriptures encourage the Christian wife and mother that she is alive in her immutable God (and He in her), in "whom there is no variation or shadow due to change" (James 1:17). Behold your unchanging God, and know the true security that results in peace!

Each day commit your study time to the Lord God, who eagerly desires that you understand His Word that you might live abundantly. Right now pause and ask God the Holy Spirit to be your Teacher.

Discovery I/God Is Changeless

There is great insecurity today due in part to the tremendous changes that seem characteristic of this century. The Bible speaks to this dilemma by declaring that *God* is always the same!

1. Why would the great proclamation of Malachi 3:6 be stabilizing for you during times of change in situations around you as well as in the midst of inner turmoil?____

   _____

   _____

2. a. When God declared His name to be _____ (Exod. 3:14), instead of I *was* or I *will* be, what was He revealing concerning His person? _____

   _____

   b. Now compare Exodus 3:14 with John 8:58. Who is speaking and what is being revealed in John 8:58?

   _____

   _____

3. Using Hebrews 13:8 as your basis, answer the following question: Does Jesus Christ love you as much right now as

when He gave up His life for you? Explain. _____

_____

_____

4. God alone possesses immortality, for He has always been and always will be; He does not change (1 Tim. 6:16). Therefore, God is the only One who could offer what "gift" to mankind (2 Tim. 1:10)? Do you possess *this* gift right now?_____

_____

5. The Old Testament writers repeatedly refer to God as *the Rock*. For a moment, reflect in your mind's eye upon a rock. List reasons why the "rock" image might have been used to portray the invisible God._____

_____

_____

_____

6. Carefully rewrite James 1:17 in your own words, making personal application of this verse to *your own life*. _____

_____

_____

Discovery II/Results of God's Immutability

7. a. Because God does not change, what *must* be true (Num. 23:19; Isa. 46:10)? ("Repenting" means to change one's plan of action.)_____

_____

_____

   b. What do these promises mean in terms of your own life?_____

_____

8. a. List the facts that can be discovered concerning the Word of God through the following verses:

   Psalm 33:11 _____

   Psalm 119:89,152 _____

   Isaiah 40:6-8 _____

   Matthew 5:17-18 _____

   b. Briefly summarize what you have discovered in these verses. _____

   _____

   _____

   c. In light of the above, what should *your attitude* be concerning the Word of God? _____

   _____

   _____

9. What is the foundational principle behind Psalm 33:11? How would you practically apply Psalm 33:11 when the counsel of God differs from that of the world's (i.e., marriage, rearing of children, business practices, church order)? _____

   _____

   _____

   _____

10. a. Because God does not change, in Psalm 100:5, what is stated as continuing forever? _____

    _____

    b. When we wonder, "Does God still love me after what I've done?" what are we actually saying about God? What have we forgotten? _____

    _____

11. In contrast to the heavens and earth, what does God declare in Isaiah 51:6 will never end? _____

_____

12. By using the attribute of power to explain your answer, show how God's nature of changelessness affects His other attributes. _____

_____

_____

Discovery III/A Biblical Example of God's Changelessness

Because God is changeless, He must always be faithful to His promises. Abraham and Sarah's adventure into parenthood beautifully illustrates this truth.

13. a. According to Genesis 11:29-30, Abram (later God changed name to Abraham) married _____, but she was _____

b. However, what was God's promise to Abram (Gen. 12:1-3)? What is implied in this promise concerning Abram and Sarai's plight? _____

_____

_____

c. How is God's promise broadened in Genesis 13:14-16, and what is now clear concerning the couple's problem? _____

_____

_____

Discovery IV/Man Struggles to Wait on God in Faith When He Cannot "See"

14. Read Genesis 15:1-6.

a. What was Abram's struggle as he interacted with God?

_____

_____

b. Can you identify with Abram by naming a struggle you are having with a promise God has given to you? ___

_____

_____

c. How did God encourage Abram? _____

_____

d. State Abram's response._____

_____

e. What is *your* present response to a promise God has given you? What should it be (Heb. 11:6)? _____

_____

_____

f. When Abram believed, was his prayer immediately answered in a way he could see (Gen. 16:1)?_____

_____

15. a. Since God didn't appear to "come through" immediately, Sarai talked Abram into helping God out. The couple took things into their own hands using the world's methods of their day. Explain the common practice of their day and the unhappiness that resulted from their use of it (Gen. 16:1-6). _____

_____

_____

b. Though often appearing easier or perhaps the only possible alternative to our problem, the ways of the world that go against God's counsel end in unhappiness. Can you give an example of a time you tried to help God out and "disaster" was the result?_____

_____

_____

_____

16. God waited as Abram and Sarai tried their way, and then He renewed and expanded His promise to them in Genesis 17:1-8. Explain how God, this time, was very specific about the promise's fulfillment (Gen. 17:21). _____

_____

_____

17. a. Read Genesis 18:1-15. Describe what is happening in this passage as if you were Sarah. _____

_____

_____

_____

 b. Did Sarah's physical state affect God's fulfilling His promises (Gen. 21:1-3)? _____

_____

 c. What reasons have you unconsciously set up as to why God cannot fulfill His promise to you? _____

_____

_____

 d. When you consider the character of God, do your "reasons" still stand? _____

_____

_____

Discovery V/What God's Changlessness Means to You

18. a. No matter how often you move to a new locale or face new circumstances, as a Christian woman, where is your real dwelling place (Ps. 90:1-2)? _____

b. Why would this "place" be secure? _____

_____

19. What is God's great encouragement and blessing to parents who humbly seek Him (Ps. 102:28)? _____

_____

20. What does Job 23:13 say about God, and what important result follows in verse 14? In terms of your life, what is God saying to you through this passage as you compare it with Psalm 18:30? _____

_____

21. Memorize Malachi 3:6 that the Holy Spirit might remind you of God's changelessness.

10

GOD IS FAITHFUL

God has declared Himself to be *faithful*. Being faithful is to be absolutely firm in adherence to promises and commitments to another.

> Know therefore that the LORD your God is God, the *faithful* God (Deut. 7:9).

We have all known the hurt of unfaithfulness. We have wondered whom we can depend on. The Scriptures answer us by coupling the truth that God is faithful with the fact that God cannot change. "For I the Lord do not change" (Mal. 3:6). God will always be faithful to you because it is impossible for Him to change. For God to be unfaithful even once would cause Him to change. God's very name is "Faithful" (Rev. 19:11), for He is perfect in faithfulness. Imagine, there *is* Someone who will never let you down, who will never break His promise to you!

What does this mean to you? God *will be, must be,* faithful to His Word and to every promise He has made to you in it:

> Faithful is he that calleth you, who also will do it (1 Thess. 5:24, KJV).

Faithful is He who calls you as encourager to your husband with his unique needs, who also will give *you* grace to meet those needs.

Faithful is He who calls you as mother to your specific children with their individual physical limitations, temperaments, and mental capacities, who will enable you to work properly with them.

Faithful is He who calls you to a seemingly impossible task, who will give you the needed ability to accomplish that task (Heb. 4:16).

Since God is perfect, He cannot fail you even once! What security, what peace, what confidence is now possible for you as a person, as a wife, as a mother, as the organizer of your home.

> I can do all things in him [Christ] who strengthens [or empowers] me (Phil. 4:13).

He is faithful—absolutely firm in His adherence to His promise to you.

Another aspect of this security in God's faithfulness rests in the fact that His faithfulness to us is not conditioned by our faithfulness to Him. "If we are faithless, he remains faithful—for he cannot deny himself" (2 Tim. 2:13). The fact that God is continually faithful to us, no matter what we do, is an important basis of our confidence in Him.

"What do you mean—God is faithful? Look at the situation I am in!"

We may not realize God's faithfulness to us at a particular point in time because of our emotions or the way things "appear" to us at the moment. But be assured, God sees the total picture, and His actions are perfect. God is at this very moment being absolutely faithful to you, for He can do nothing else.

Faith in—giving mental assent to—God's faithfulness will result in security and inner peace. Despite our emotions or what the surrounding circumstances seem to tell us, our confident mental assent (faith) rests in the fact that *God is faithful*. What can rock us? We stand confident, peaceful, secure. Are you worried, discouraged, afraid, or tempted? Be encouraged; God is faithful to *you*.

> But this I call to mind, and therefore I have hope: The steadfast love of the LORD never ceases, his mercies never come to an end; they are new every morning; great is thy faithfulness. "The LORD is my portion," says my soul, "therefore I will hope *in Him*" (Lam. 3:21-24).

Discovery I/God's Faithfulness Gives Hope

1. This week memorize Lamentations 3:21-24.
2. a. When the prophet Jeremiah is at the point of despair at the bottom of an emotional as well as a literal pit (Lam. 3:1-20), what does he call to mind that encourages him and gives him hope (Lam. 3:21-24)?_____

   _____

   _____

   b. Why would the statement "Great is Thy faithfulness" be particularly significant for Jeremiah to remember at this time when his situation was dismal?_____

   _____

   _____

   c. Upon what had Jeremiah's mind been dwelling, and with what result (Lam. 3:19-20)? Do you ever do this? What is usually the result?_____

   _____

   _____

3. When you are discouraged and feel that God may have forgotten you, what has God given as a reminder that He *will* be continually faithful to you (Gen. 8:22)? _____

4. Upon what basis can Paul make his powerful declaration in 2 Timothy 1:12? What must *you* realize about God before you can also make this statement? _____

_____

_____

5. a. No matter what the current cultural fad is concerning the good or "free" way to live, the commandments of God are _____

   and _____
   (Ps. 119:129-130, and especially 137-138).

   b. Why would understanding this truth about the commands of God be stabilizing for you in a world of changing theories concerning such things as marriage, the raising of children, and the way to peace of mind?

   _____

   _____

6. Rewrite the amazing truth of 2 Timothy 2:13 in words specifically related to you. _____

_____

_____

7. What do the following verses state that Jesus Christ will do; and therefore, what are they saying about Him (2 Thess. 3:3; Heb. 2:17; Rev. 19:11)? _____

_____

_____

Discovery II/God's Specific Faithfulness to You

8. In each of the following verses indicate what God says He will be faithful to do *for you*. As you write out your answers, apply each personally to your life.

   a. 1 Corinthians 1:9 _____

   _____

   b. 1 Corinthians 10:13_____

   _____

   c. 2 Thessalonians 3:3_____

   _____

   d. 2 Timothy 2:13_____

   _____

   e. 1 John 1:9 _____

   _____

9. According to Psalm 91:4, what is God's faithfulness to be to you? What do you think is meant by this phrase in terms of your own life? (A dictionary may help.) _____

   _____

   _____

10. Think of an issue that is present in your life. Has God made any promise in His Word that would relate to this issue? If so, what is it? How could the realization that God is absolutely faithful in His promises encourage you now?

   _____

   _____

   _____

11. Describe some of the ways God has demonstrated His faithfulness to you personally. _____

_____

_____

_____

12. At least once a day this week, meditate on the fact that *God is faithful to you*. Explain briefly what this truth means in light of your unique responsibilities as a wife:_____

_____

_____

your responsibilities as a mother: _____

_____

_____

Discovery III/God's Unchanging Faithfulness

The biblical account of Abraham and Sarah becoming parents demonstrates not only God's immutability (see "God Is Immutable"), but also God's faithfulness to accomplish what He has promised.

13. In Hebrews 11:11, what attribute of God was of special encouragement to Sarah to believe God's promise? (It is important to note that the object of Abraham and Sarah's faith was not God's promise alone, but their faith rested in the character of God Himself.) God's Word is faithful because God is faithful! _____

_____

14. a. When everything around you appears to belie God's faithfulness to His promises, what are you to do according to Isaiah 50:10? _____

_____

b. What are you to remember (John 13:17)? _____

_____

_____

15. a. Name some reasons why you might not be aware of God's faithfulness to you. _____

_____

_____

_____

   b. When you make a decision to accept the witness of these "reasons" over the witness of Scripture, in what are you placing faith? _____

_____

16. Is it possible for God to be unfaithful to you even once? Explain. _____

_____

_____

17. When you are going through suffering not of your own making, what are you to do (1 Peter 4:19)? _____

_____

Discovery IV/You, a Faithful Person

18. a. What does Luke 16:10 indicate is true of a faithful person? _____

_____

   b. In what areas of your life is this true or becoming true of you? _____

_____

_____

   c. Can you think of areas in which you feel particularly unfaithful? Explain. _____

_____

_____

d. Do you want to become a person characterized by faithfulness?_____

_____

e. When you become a Christian (by believing that Jesus Christ died for your sins and rose from the dead that you might live in newness of life), the Scriptures declare the Spirit of God comes to live within you. What "fruit of the Spirit" in Galatians 5:22-23 applies to your desire to become a faithful person? According to these verses, how do you become faithful? _____

_____

_____

19. a. Name an area in which you desire to be faithful:

   to God _____

   to your husband _____

   to your children _____

   to your friends_____

   b. Now talk to God about these areas. Thank Him that He who is faithful lives in *you*, giving you His faithfulness to make *you* faithful in these areas.

   c. As you respond to this challenge, what is important to remember when you "feel" you never could change (2 Cor. 5:7)?_____

   _____

11

GOD IS HOLY

"Holy, holy, holy is the LORD of hosts" (Isa. 6:3).

A vissionary picture of the holiness of God accompanied God's commissioning services of the prophets. The resulting concept of the holiness of God in the prophets' hearts became their stability in desperate times. No matter what the pressure, these men stood firm, for they knew their God, that He is holy!

The central truth behind the purity and honor of all the attributes of God is that God is "majestic in holiness" (Exod. 15:11). Therefore, the Scriptures refer to the holiness of God more than to any other attribute.

If we would begin to understand what "God is holy" means, we, too, would become strong and greatly rejoice and "bless His holy name" (Ps. 103:1). However, *holy* is just a word until we have a concept or picture to give it meaning.

The basic meaning of the word *holy* is "to cut" or "to separate." When *holy* is used in reference to God, it refers to

His total separation from evil. Not even a hint of a blemish could be found in our God; He is completely pure. "God is light and in him is no darkness at all" (1 John 1:5).

What an encouragement to us who trust in *His name* to realize that not the slightest evil blemish or flaw could ever be found in God's nature of love, sovereignty, power, wisdom, faithfulness, goodness, etc., because *He is holy*. As with all His attributes, this absolute purity, this total separation from evil, is effortless for God. There is no struggle to be or to maintain holiness; He simply is holy and cannot be otherwise.

"Who shall not fear and glorify thy name, O Lord? For thou alone art holy" (Rev. 15:4).

Because God is holy, He hates sin and must judge it. God would be denying His very character were it possible for Him to overlook sin. The cross of Jesus Christ (when God allowed the full vengeance of His wrath against sin to be poured out upon His very own Son) is evidence that sin must be punished. Apart from Jesus Christ and His finished work on the cross, there can be *no* hope of holiness for us. But, joy of unbeliev- able joys, we are "accepted in the beloved" and receive God's righteousness (Eph. 1:6) when we believe in Jesus Christ as our Savior from sin's power and judgment. (God's righteousness is what makes us acceptable to God.)

Holiness may seem a strange, almost negative, concept to us because we have become conditioned all our lives to accept that which is marred by sin and is thus unholy. Since we live with unholiness daily, we are more shocked by purity. The idea of holiness bewilders us. The holiness of God seems a lofty but unrelated-to-life concept for the theologian to medi- tate upon—but for the diaper-washing, floor-scrubbing housewife, what is its relevancy?

The Scriptures answer us:

> Acquaint now thyself with him (God—that he is holy) and *be at peace* (Job 22:21, KJV).

Holiness is relevant to peace!

> The [women] who know their God (that he is holy) shall stand firm and take action (Dan. 11:32).

Holiness is relevant to strength!

> You will know the truth (that our God is Holy), and the truth will make you free (John 8:32).

Holiness is relevant to freedom!

> Knowledge of the Holy is understanding (Prov. 9:10, KJV).

Holiness is relevant to understanding!

But there is more! Holiness is relevant to the concept of true beauty and freedom. Holiness is at the core of beauty and freedom, for these are the result when evil is absent or has been cut away.

"The beauty of the LORD" (Ps. 27:4) is also referred to as "the beauty of holiness" (Ps. 110:3). The beauty of holiness is the natural majestic beauty brilliantly present when evil is absent (e.g., the Garden of Eden before the Fall, our glorified bodies, etc.). Consider, for an earthly example, a sparkling mountain stream fed by melting snow. This picture stands in sharp contrast to the ugliness of a stagnant, murky pond filled with smelly waste and soiled food wrappers.

It is with the beauty of holiness that we, as Christian women, are to be "adorned" (1 Tim. 2:8-11). This adornment is not dependent on bank accounts or physical endowments, but is the beauty that continually glows from a life liberated from sin, set apart from evil. The Scriptures declare *this adornment is to be ours* as women in Christ.

The freedom of holiness is the inner freedom experienced in a life separated from bitterness, selfishness, envy, covetousness, and putrifying habits. The beauty and freedom of holiness is demonstrated by lives "no longer [lived] for themselves but for him who for their sake died and was raised" (2 Cor. 5:15).

God alone stands separate from evil; He alone can be the Source of all Holiness; and He is alive in you, the Christian woman! In Christ, He has cleansed you from all evil and has given you His Holy Spirit to accomplish holiness in you. Therefore, God can command you (for your good and to make you radiantly beautiful and truly free). "Be ye holy; for I am holy" (1 Peter 1:16, KJV).

When God lives in you "glorious in holiness," He may call you to joyfully "worship the LORD in the beauty of holiness" (1 Chron. 16:29, KJV).

Discovery I/Holy Is the Lord!

1. *Who* is holy and what does this holiness demand from you (1 Sam. 2:2; Rev. 15:4)?_____

   _____

   _____

2. In your own words, explain the word *holy* as it is used in reference to God (the introductory section may help you).

   _____

   _____

3. a. Using a dictionary to help you, define the word *glorious.*_____

   _____

   _____

   b. In Exodus 15:11, discover what it is that makes God "glorious." Explain why this is true. _____

   _____

   _____

4. a. When God spoke to His people, Israel, He referred to Himself over and over again as the "Holy One of Israel." Why do you think God sought to emphasize this attribute to His people? _____

_____

_____

b. Why would it be good for *you* to remember God's holiness? _____

_____

_____

c. Psalm 30:4 commands us to do what at the remembrance of God's holiness?_____

_____

d. Write out "God alone is holy" (Rev. 15:4) and put these words in a place where you'll see them in order to remind yourself of this truth every day this week. Also, be obedient to God's specific command found in Psalm 30:4.

5. a. Because God is holy, according to Psalm 93:5 and Isaiah 57:15, what is characteristic of God's house?

_____

b. How does this truth relate to you as a Christian in a practical way when you compare it with 1 Corinthians 3:16-17?_____

_____

_____

Discovery II/The Holy Lamb of God

6. What special names are given to Jesus Christ in Acts 3:13-15? _____

_____

_____

7. a. When a sacrifice for forgiveness of sin was made during Old Testament times, what type of offering did God require (Lev. 4:32-35)? _____

_____

b. What truth do you think God was trying to picture through this sacrifice? _____

_____

_____

c. How do John 1:29 and 1 Peter 1:18-19 refer to Jesus Christ? _____

_____

d. In what way do Hebrews 9:12-14 and 1 Peter 1:18-19 set forth evidence that Jesus Christ is holy? _____

_____

_____

Discovery III/The Only Basis for a Relationship With God

8. According to Scripture, has any human being been holy and so able to approach a holy God (Rom. 3:10,23)?

_____

9. a. Do you think it would be possible for God to compromise His holy character in order to "overlook" your sin? Why or why not?_____

_____

_____

b. If this were the end of the story here, what one word would you use to describe the plight of man?_____

_____

10. a. What unbelievable thing has our holy God done to solve our problem of unholiness and so enable a personal relationship with Him to be possible (Isa. 53; Rom. 5:6,8-9; Eph. 1:7)?_____

_____

11. From your discoveries in this section, explain the basis for the truths found in John 14:6 and 1 John 5:11-12. ____

_____

_____

12. a. How do we receive the righteousness of God so that we might approach God (Rom. 3:22)? _____

_____

   b. How must *you* respond before you can be accepted by a holy God?_____

_____

   c. If this has been, or now is, your response, what miraculous thing becomes true of you (Isa. 53:11; Col. 1:22)?

_____   ____

_____

Discovery IV/God's Liberating Purpose for You

13. a. What amazing adventure is now possible *for you* because of Ephesians 1:7; Colossians 1:22; and Hebrews 4:16? Be sure to personalize your answer. ____

_____

   b. What is my heart attitude to be as I come to God (Isa. 57:15)?_____

_____

14. In light of Ephesians 1:3-4; 2 Timothy 1:9; and 1 Peter 1:16, what overall purpose did God have in choosing *you*? (Put your own name in these verses as you read them.)_____

_____

_____

15. One of God's clear purposes for the Christian woman is to become beautiful. Let's consider the following in order to understand this concept more fully.

   a. According to the following verses, what constitutes "beauty" in God's presence (Exod. 28:2; Ps. 96:6,9)?

   _____

   b. Though women try many different ways to become "beautiful," what is *God's way,* as seen through 1 Timothy 2:9-10; 1 Peter 1:16; and 1 Peter 3:3-5?

   _____

   _____

16. a. Thinking about specific areas in your life, what possible results might you expect from the application of 1 Peter 1:16 into your life?_____

   _____

   _____

   b. Discover two things God has done to make this command possible in your life (Col. 1:21-22). (Remember: God has always provided everything necessary to enable you to carry out His commands.) _____

   _____

   _____

Discovery V/Experiencing God's Holiness

17. How does holiness become experiential in you personally (Rom. 12:1-2; 2 Cor. 7:1; 1 Thess. 3:12-13; and Heb. 12:10)?_____

   _____

   _____

18. In what way is a "holier-than-thou" attitude the opposite from the holy heart-attitude that is so acceptable to God (Ps. 51:17; Isa. 66:2b)? _____

_____

_____

19. Those who will see the Lord are those who are _____ and _____ (Heb. 12:14).

20. Memorize 1 John 1:5 and Revelation 15:4.

12

GOD IS JUST

To live life as God meant us to live—with inner peace, freedom, and joy, no matter what the circumstances, we must *know* God that we might *trust in* and *call upon* His name. We have been learning together the names of God: Love, Sovereign, All-Powerful, All-Knowing, All-Wisdom, Always Present, Unchanging, Faithful, and Holy.

"Right!" we say with conviction. But His name is also *Justice,* and therefore, His holy justice (wrath) must fall against sin, both external sin and the silent sin of heart attitude.

"Oh, dear," we think, "did you have to bring that up?" Even as Christian women, we may wince when the justice of God comes under discussion. A God of goodness and love is popular; but at the mention of a God of justice, people get "turned off," and secretly we may also. "How can perfect love, goodness, *and justice* exist together?" we may ask. When we ask, we have forgotten that God is holy.

Our concept of the justice of God may be weak because our

view of love and goodness is so flawed, so "unholy" (see "God Is Holy"). We are so conditioned to rationalize or flirt with sin that it almost seems the kind thing to do, and thus we expect it of God. "You thought that I was one like yourself" (Ps. 50:21). But God is perfectly holy, and therefore, He alone knows what life is like without sin. Knowing the indescribable joy of holiness, no wonder our God hates sin with holy hatred and anger; for sin maims, rots, and destroys His creation mentally, emotionally, and physically. Since God loves perfectly and desires only good for His children, how could He look with indifference upon the destructive power of sin?

If we as mothers could realize the destruction that sin is presently working in our child's life and the future tragic results of that sin, wouldn't our anger burn against it? Wouldn't we be motivated to rise from our comfortable seat of apathy to correct our child in loving, consistent discipline that would not compromise? Especially this is a lesson to us "tender-hearted" mothers who have toddlers we consider too young to understand or perhaps little ones with physical problems. Our God of love tells us clearly, "He who spares the rod hates his son, but he who loves him is diligent to discipline him" (Prov. 13:24). Truly goodness and love without justice is not good or loving.

The holiness of God means that He can never accept sin even though "he knows our frame; He remembers that we are dust" (Ps. 103:14). Justice is God's stand against sin. "For the wrath of God is revealed from heaven against all ungodliness and unrighteousness of men" (Rom. 1:18).

The holy anger of God against the awfulness of sin was displayed in the Garden of Eden when both man and woman chose to act independently from God. Again God's judgment was seen through the Flood, the destruction of Sodom and Gomorrah, and surely it should be against us, our husbands, and our children, for we are sinful (Rom. 3:23)! God is just; sin must be punished. *But, because of God's great love for us,* His most terrible judgment against sin was meted out upon *His own Son,* Jesus Christ. He took the judgment we were to have. Was this easy for Christ? Consider the anguished response of Jesus Christ as the wrath of the almighty God was unleashed upon Him.

> My God, my God, why hast thou forsaken me? . . . Yet thou art holy" (Ps. 22:1,3).

He who had known only holiness now experienced the horror of sin. And not only this, but on the cross, God the Son experienced the awful wrath of God which none other could have stood. "The wicked will not stand in the judgment" (Ps. 1:5).

Perfect love, goodness, and justice *do* exist together and have been unbelievably displayed to us at the cross. This amazing truth should give cause for rejoicing no matter your present situation, for:

> Jesus who delivers us from the wrath to come (1 Thess. 1:10).

> There is therefore now *no* condemnation for those who are in Christ Jesus. For the law of the Spirit of life in Christ Jesus has set me free from the law of sin and death (Rom. 8:1-2).

Discovery I/God's Justice

The words *justice* and *righteousness* are used interchangeably in Scripture.

1. Look up the word *justice* in the dictionary, and write out a brief definition._____

   _____

2. a. Read Deuteronomy 32:3-4. Explain the phrase "all his ways are justice" in light of your definition of *justice.*

   _____

   _____

3. How does the Scripture describe God's judgments in the following verses:

   a. Psalm 119:137 _____

   b. Psalm 145:17 _____

4. a. As you reflect on Psalm 89:14, what do you think is meant by the statement: "Righteousness and justice are the *foundation of thy throne*"? _____

   _____

   _____

   b. Explain Psalm 89:15-16 in a way that would relate these verses very personally to your life. (Putting your own name into the verse will help you.) _____

   _____

   _____

5. a. Name the three things Zephaniah 3:5 declares that the Lord will do. _____

   _____

   _____

   _____

   b. What is God saying through these verses to you personally

      1) In respect to your marriage?_____

      _____

      _____

      2) in light of a difficult relationship?_____

      _____

      _____

Discovery II/Jesus Christ

6. How is Jesus Christ prophetically described in Zechariah

9:9? _____

_____

_____

7. a. How did the man who allowed Jesus to be led off to crucifixion refer to Jesus (Matt. 27:24)? _____

_____

  b. Who will be the world's righteous judge at the end time (2 Thess. 1:7-9; Rev. 6:16)?_____

_____

  c. How does Jesus Himself describe His judgments in John 5:30?_____

_____

8. a. Who is being described in the song of Revelation 15:3-4? Compare with John 1:29,35-36. _____

_____

  b. How is this One described? _____

_____

_____

  c. As you meditate on the fact that this same One so desires a relationship *with you*, what does this passage mean to you personally?_____

_____

_____

9. a. Because God is just, what can you be certain He will do (Deut. 32:43; Acts 17:31; Rom. 1:18; 2 Thess. 1:6-9)? _____

_____

_____

  b. Yet, what is God's desire (1 Tim. 2:4-6)?_____

_____

10. What question does Job 9:2 ask that 1 Peter 3:18 answers? How does this relate to you? _____

_____

_____

11. As a believer in Jesus Christ, what is *now* true of you personally?

a. Romans 3:26 _____

b. Romans 5:1 _____

c. Romans 5:9 _____

d. Romans 8:1 _____

e. 1 Thessalonians 1:10 _____

12. How is the just (or justified) woman to live each day (Rom. 1:17; Gal. 2:20; Hos. 14:9)? Make a decision to live this way *today,* especially in an area troublesome to you. _____

_____

_____

13. Because God is just, what will He do for you as a woman who believes in Christ as your Savior (Ps. 94:12; Heb. 12:7-11; 1 John 1:9)? _____

_____

_____

Discovery III/The Commandments of the Lord Are Just

God freed us from sin by the cross of Jesus Christ. He then gave His Holy Spirit to empower us to live holy lives. God has given us His Word that we might know the truth.

14. What constructive thing does the psalmist do to keep sin from controlling him (Ps. 119:11)? _____

_____

15. Study Psalm 19:7-11

    a. List at least *seven* words that are used to describe the commandments (statutes) of the Lord God. _____

    _____

    _____

    _____

    b. Discover *five* results that will take place in your life as you follow His commands._____

    _____

    _____   _____

    _____

    c. Are you interested in experiencing these "results" *in your life?* According to Psalm 19, what does that mean that you must do?_____

    _____

    _____

Discovery IV/An Encouragement to Be Just

16. a. What does the realization of the justice of God motivate us to do if our husbands and children do not know the Lord, or if they are disobedient to His Word (2 Cor. 5:11)?_____

    _____

    b. According to the Scriptures, what is the best way a wife may "encourage" her husband in God's ways (1 Peter 3:1-4)? _____

    _____

    _____

    c. How are we to encourage our children to faith in God (Deut. 6:6-7)? _____

_____

_____

17. What is God's promise to those who are just?

   a. Proverbs 3:33 _____

   b. Proverbs 4:18 _____

   c. Proverbs 10:6 _____

   d. Proverbs 10:20 _____

   e. Proverbs 10:31 _____

   f. Proverbs 12:13 _____

   g. Proverbs 20:7 _____

18. What is the challenge of the holy God to you, His daughter, as seen in 2 Chronicles 19:7? List three specific ways you could begin to implement this challenge today. ____

_____

_____

_____

_____

19. Memorize Deuteronomy 32:4.

13

PRAISE THE LORD

Have you ever had the following experience? You are greatly burdened or overwhelmed. Perhaps your husband has lost his job or a loved one is in trouble; maybe you're anxious about an illness, or someone has wronged you. You bring your situation to the Lord, saying, "Here, Lord, is my problem; I commit it to You." After your prayer is finished, the first thought that pops into you head is your burden!

Perhaps you are the strong type who by sheer determination tries hard not to think of a committed problem, saying over and over, "Lord, it's Yours; it's Yours!" But what slides back into your mind to be meditated on as you comb your hair or do dishes—the misery of your circumstances. You repeat the committing cycle till you are exasperated, finally feeling guilty that you are not a stronger Christian. You note, however, that during the whole process your mental attitude concerning your situation has not altered.

There is a command in the Scriptures that speaks to this

dilemma. It speaks as plainly to the overwhelming events of your life as it does to daily circumstances, such as being discouraged or "kind of down" for no apparent reason, anxious or tense over your schedule, irritated at the unexpected, or frustrated by disappointed hopes.

The command of God that relates very practically to daily life yet perhaps has been reserved for only " special moments is the command to *praise the Lord*. The importance of this command is emphasized by the fact that it is mentioned more often than any other in the Old Testament. It seems that God does not want us to overlook or forget to praise Him. The heart cry of the psalmist David leads us to this same conclusion: "Oh that men would praise the Lord for his goodness, and for his wonderful works to the children of men!" (Ps. 107:8, KJV). However, to praise we must learn about God's person. Therefore, it is within the context of a study of the character of God that the command to praise the Lord is best understood.

Since the command to praise the Lord is so vital to our lives as Christians, let us examine it. At the same time, we will be answering the question often asked at the conclusion of a study series, "How do I remember and then apply what I've learned?" In terms of this study, the answer is "Praise the Lord." Praise keeps the character of God before our minds. The practice of praise forces us to relate God's character to the issues of life. The effect of praising God on our mental attitude is liberating, for praise focuses our attention on the person and work of God.

Discovery I/The Commands of God

1. Why has God given you specific commands in His word (Deut. 5:29; Pss. 18:30; 32:8)? _____

   _____

   _____

2. Give an example of a command of God that has been a

particular blessing to you. Illustrate._____

_____

_____

_____

3. Name the command that is specified in such verses as Psalms 106:1; 135:1-3; 147:1; and 148:1._____

_____

Discovery II/Why Praise?

Why are we given the command to praise the Lord? Is praise something reserved for special moments in church or only to be done by those who have reached a certain point of spiritual maturity? Praising the Lord may sound like a "super-spiritual" activity having little practical relevance to everyday life. Yet, we will see it is to be at the core of our new life as a Christian.

4. According to the Scriptures, why are we to praise the Lord?

a. Deuteronomy 5:29_____

b. Psalm 33:1 _____

c. Psalm 50:23 _____

d. Psalm 147:1 _____

5. Through praise we can experience inner joy, peace, and freedom in the midst of difficult circumstances, for the praise of God focuses our attention on God's person; and then we may view our circumstances with new perspective. Acts 16:16-34 is an excellent example of this aspect of praise.

a. Briefly describe the external situation facing Paul and Silas._____

_____

_____

b. What do you think would be the natural human response to such circumstances?_____

_____

_____

c. In contrast, what are Paul and Silas doing in the midst of their difficult circumstances (Acts 16:25)?_____

_____

d. In light of this passage, what do you think was Paul and Silas' perspective concerning their situation?_____

_____

_____

Discovery III/What Is Praise?

The basic meaning of the word *praise* is "confession in the sense of a declaration."

6. What is to be the subject of biblical praise according to Deuteronomy 10:21?_____

_____

We see, then, that praise is not saying, "Praise the Lord. Praise the Lord," over and over again; for that is but the imperative call to do it. In Deuteronomy 10:21, we discover that praise is to center on God, emphasizing:

    a) who God is—"He is your praise."
    b) what He has done—"Who has done for you these great and terrible things."

To summarize: The praise of God is the declaration or confession to yourself or others of who God is and what He has done.

7. Have you ever looked at a beautiful sunset, longing to do something in response, but not knowing what to do? God

has created mankind with the innate desire to praise and has stated in His Word the only way to fulfill that desire. However, if man doesn't praise God, he will seek to praise something else.

a. Explain what that "something" might be, using Daniel 5:23 to help you with your answer. _____

_____

_____

b. Why do you think this type of praise would be empty?

_____

_____

c. Applying Daniel 5:23 to our day, what types of things are praised in our culture? _____

_____

_____

8. In response to the deadness of Daniel 5:23, what does the Lord, through the psalmist David, cry out for us to do in Psalms 65:1; 107:8,15,21,31-32? _____

_____

Discovery IV/How Are We to Praise?

The call to praise is the call to remember what our God is like—what His name is—and what He has done because of His name. Praise will remind or encourage us to put our trust in God no matter what the circumstances.

As with all the commands of God, obedience to the command to praise the Lord will result in blessing (Deut. 5:29). Sincere praise will always affect your mental attitude in that it alters the focus of your attention from the situation to God.

Though circumstances must be faced realistically, as illustrated in the Psalms, circumstances are not to be (as they all too often are) our meditation. Our minds are to dwell on the character of God (Ps. 42:11).

9. How are we to praise the Lord?

   a. Psalm 9:1_____

   b. Psalm 34:1 _____

   c. Psalm 47:7 _____

   d. Summarize your conclusions into a sentence using your own name (*example:* Mary will . . .). _____

_____

   What are we to do when we praise the Lord? The Scripture reveals two basic ways praise is to be given.

10. *Descriptive praise:* the describing or declaring of the character or attributes of God in a general way with no specific situation in mind.

   a. Illustrate how Psalm 145 is an example of descriptive praise by listing the various attributes of God mentioned. List the verse along with each attribute. ____

     _____

     _____

     _____

     _____

     _____

   b. Can you give a personal example of a specific time you reminded yourself of various aspects of God's character? What was the effect of this *praise* on your mental attitude?_____

     _____

     _____

     _____

11. *Declarative praise:* declaring what God has done in a

specific situation or for a specific person. For example: God has been faithful to meet Mary's need as a new mother. In the emergency, He gave her wisdom to know what to do for her baby.

a. Demonstrate how Psalm 30 is an example of declarative praise. _____

_____

_____

_____

b. Give an illustration from your own life of what God has specifically done for you that demonstrates an aspect of His character. _____

_____

_____

_____

Discovery V/Two Women Who Knew How to Praise

Two mothers in Scripture are examples to us of women who knew how to praise the Lord and did so. The Scriptures reveal that both faced a humanly difficult situation with the attitude of praise to God.

12. Read 1 Samuel 1:1-28.

a. State the human difficulty faced by Hannah, the mother of the prophet Samuel (1 Sam. 1:24-28). ___

_____

_____

b. In one word, what was Hannah's response? _____

_____

13. a. In Luke 1:26-38 and Matthew 1:18-19, what difficulty did Mary, the mother of Jesus, face? _____

_____

b. How did she respond to her circumstances? _____

14. Choose either (or both for a special challenge and blessing) the praise statements of Hannah (1 Sam. 2:1-10) or Mary's song of praise (Luke 1:46-55), and discover and list the attributes of God mentioned in the passage (use verses to support each). State, if you can, what type of praise each is, descriptive or declarative. _____

_____

_____

_____

_____

15. Why do you think the remembrance of God's character would have been of encouragement to these women?

_____

_____

16. Applying the command to praise the Lord to your life:
    a. Can you think of a difficult or pressure situation you are now facing? According to the Scriptures, what should you do for your own good (Ps. 42:11)? _____

    _____

    _____

    b. Whether you are in a difficult situation or not, *when* are you to praise (Ps. 34:1)? In what ways would obedience to Psalm 34:1 affect your life? _____

    _____

    _____

    _____

17. The praise of God is to be done continually with understanding and whole-heartedly, but sometimes you just don't feel like praising. Because God knows the blessing that will result from praise, He asks you to make praise _____(Heb. 13:15).

Praise leads you to *behold your God!*

SUGGESTIONS FOR LEADERS

The leader's role in guiding the discussion group is a very important one. The primary goal of the discussion leader is not to teach, but to lead the discussion so that the participants are encouraged to share discoveries from their own study. This sharing is a necessary part of the learning process. It is a wise leader's job to make sure this happens by—

1. Trusting the Holy Spirit of God to work through them;

2. Providing a warm atmosphere where all are encouraged to share;

3. Keeping the discussion "on track" not allowing it to go off on a tangent. The discussion must not be based upon what people think, but upon what the Word of God says. The weekly questions are designed to keep the discussion on the Scriptures. The leader may always ask, "How did you answer the next question?" and so move the group on through the material.

4. Attempting to cover all the assigned material. This moti-

vates and encourages the participants to finish the week's study.

5. Maintaining a rule that only those who have done the assigned material may share. This also encourages and motivates the participants to complete their lesson prior to the discussion time.

6. Shortening or rephrasing the questions when necessary for the sake of time or interest.

7. Varying your method. Some questions will lend themselves to sharing around the group circle, each one giving part of the answer. For other questions, an answer from one person might be sufficient. At times it may be broadening to have varied observations from several on the same question.

SUGGESTIONS FOR LECTURE LEADERS

The teacher's lecture should include—

1. Making sure the attribute of God is properly understood;

2. Drawing applications from the week's material that specifically relates to the group's needs, i.e., common situations members of the group face.

Perhaps the Introductory section of each chapter could be used as an outline for a lecture summary over the material.